ADVERTISING

IS DEAD

LONG LIVE ADVERTISING!

TOM HIMPE
foreword by Will Collin
with 435 colour illustrations

Thames & Hudson

First published in the United Kingdom in 2006 by
Thames & Hudson Ltd, 181A High Holborn, London WC1V 7QX

www.thamesandhudson.com

First paperback edition 2008

British Library Cataloguing-in-Publication Data
A catalogue record for this book is available from the British Library
ISBN 978-0-500-28687-6

Printed and bound in China by C&C Offset

'Let the battle commence.'
This slogan for a guerrilla
campaign by *The Guardian*
(see p. 69) could just as easily
be applied to today's advertising
landscape in general.

Foreword

'Has the advertising industry gone mad?'
by Will Collin, founding partner of Naked Communications

Crushed cars on street corners to advertise a movie; students paid to have a mobile phone brand logo shaved into their hair; a nude image of a female model projected onto London's Houses of Parliament to promote a magazine. We would be forgiven for thinking that the advertising industry had lost its scruples, never mind its senses.

What's behind the recent proliferation of these unconventional forms of advertising? Why is it that brands are turning to guerrilla tactics, stunts, ambient media and stealth marketing?

The reason can be traced back to the huge changes that have taken place in the way we consume media since the mid 1990s. On one hand, the arrival of multi-channel television has fragmented our viewing habits, while on the other, such new technologies as the Web and mobile and instant messaging have changed our relationship with media from passive to active.

Advertisers, therefore, can no longer rely on consumers to behave like the passive receivers they once were. We are harder to pin down, more demanding, less predictable.

So professionals have responded by looking for new forms of communication that are more noticeable and that engage with consumers more actively than the mass communication of old. Often this means finding ways for us to discover the message rather than forcing it upon us. By harnessing our natural curiosity for surprising new forms of communication, brands are compensating for the declining impact of traditional advertising.

The ad industry has not gone mad. Acting a little crazy is now the sanest thing to do.

Introduction

Getting out of the traffic jam

How long do you sit in a traffic jam before you decide to take an alternative route? As your body grows slowly numb, your mind weighs up the pros and cons. If you are not familiar with the alternative routes, you may end up losing even more time than you would in the traffic jam. And who says the other routes aren't blocked as well? Aren't they less well signposted and therefore less able to guide you clearly towards your destination? Maybe the jam you're in now will magically clear up?

As you slowly inch along, these thoughts flash through your brain. But, in the end, most of us stay put. The certainty and familiarity of the highway — it will get you to your destination eventually — is better than the unpredictability and uncertainty of a new route. Only those who know their way around, who have knowledge and experience of the other routes, will happily swap the highways for the roads less travelled.

In much the same way, conventional advertising channels — television, radio, magazines, newspapers, billboards — are blocked because too many advertisers are using the same channels to reach the same people at the same time. As a result, these channels suffer from severe and recurring traffic jams, which means a spiral of ever-decreasing efficiency: it takes more time, more money and more effort than ever before to obtain the desired effect through conventional media. Twenty years ago, just three commercials would reach 80% of the USA population. Today it takes 150[1]. The reasons are diverse and include media fragmentation, the loss of a captive audience, the rise of ad-skipping technology, the interruptive nature of conventional advertising and an increasingly ad-literate audience.

Yet, alternative routes are available. The problem is, few brands are truly aware of how to get away from the traditional channels and plunge into this new territory. The alternatives are not as fully developed, are less clearly indicated and not nearly as familiar. But that could be just what's so great about them: the freedom they bring. It might take a bit longer in terms of sheer distance travelled, but it's a joy to be able to drive, rather than sit around. As long as

brands take different alternative routes, they can make use of unique and exclusive ways to get to their destination.

Traffic jams, whether on the highway or within the media landscape, are a waste of human talent, skill, time and energy. They prevent brands from reaching their desired destination or target group. The challenge for today's advertisers and agencies is to get familiar with 'the other routes'. Only by trying them out can advertisers gain knowledge about them and feel more confident about their decision to use them.

The joys of fusion cuisine

It used to be simple. If a company had something to say, they merely came up with an ad that communicated the message and then flooded the mass media channels. The plain truth now is that such a conventional advertising recipe is as insufficient as it is predictable.

A set menu of conventional media no longer gets the point across. The formula has lost its ability to come out of nowhere and catch us off guard. Its traditional advantage — that it was an easy, familiar recipe, tested and approved by previous generations and offering a degree of certainty — seems more like a handicap today.

Advertising has become too much like fast food: convenient, without the variety and 'wow' factor of good cooking. **Communication today needs to have more in common with the experimentation of fusion cuisine and less with the predictability of pre-packaged ready meals.**

The dramatic increase in the use of alternative solutions over the last few years has helped to break down the belief that there is a golden formula, a sure and certain standard, a routine practice when it comes to brand communication. The best cure for predictability is to renounce routine practice; not to stay between the lines, but to go wild again; not to go where people expect, but where they don't; not to choose media that are abundantly used, but to find ones that have never been considered. This is what is happening today. The advertising industry has entered its adolescence, where it's OK to go and experiment with everything. This urge for experimentation has unleashed a new spectrum of possibilities capable of reaching people in more relevant, more surprising and more appropriate ways. There is, in short, a renaissance of creative ideas breathing new life into a sector that was in dire need of it.

So far, the energy generated by these experiments is raw and unfinished. Yet we can catch a glimpse of what tomorrow might bring. These experiments ensure that relationships with consumers stay fresh and lively. And, as always in a changing industry, the advertisers, the communication agencies, the media networks and the research companies that learn to harness the madness and control the experiments will be the ones who succeed – both today and tomorrow.

Advertising that deviates from traditional routes risks being perceived as intrusive and aggressive. Yet when it is done in a surprising and relevant way, as in this sperm demonstration against Durex, the consumer's full attention is captured and it could even result in a smile (see p. 156).

Choosing techniques and media

The four drivers of alternative advertising

The most reliable way to make sure you reach your destination is to have an in-depth knowledge of the available routes. Over the last few years, there has been an explosion of alternative routes in the communications industry. Terms like guerrilla, ambient, stealth, buzz, word of mouth, viral, grassroots, ambush, stunt, product placement, branded content, branded entertainment, advergaming, experiential, permission and wildfire have enjoyed increasing popularity. The vocabulary alone gives you an idea of how many forms alternative communications can take. Such labels as 'non-conventional' or 'alternative' have been used mostly as vague umbrella terms to cover the unexplored terrain beyond traditional advertising turf. Although the possibilities are endless once you venture off the well-trodden path, a number of recurring themes can be seen clearly among all the experimentation. To be more specific, the new ways in which companies are connecting with consumers have four driving forces in common: the desire for proximity, exclusivity, invisibility and unpredictability.

Proximity

Exclusivity

Invisibility

Unpredictability

Measuring the value of a medium

The amplification effect

Proximity or getting up close and personal

One of the crucial motivating factors in the relationship between brands and their customers is the desire for proximity. Companies want to get as close as possible to the point of purchase, to the moment of purchase, to the consumer's natural environment, to his or her inner circle. Yet, traditional media channels rarely offer this degree of intimacy. **Conventional media, such as television, radio, newspapers and magazines, only allow consumers and brands to meet each other 'in the middle'.**

BRAND → MEDIA ← CONSUMER

Mass media need to satisfy two different searches from two different kinds of people: the advertisers' search for a public and the people's search for information and entertainment. Media channels have united these two searches in a somewhat artificial way: by inserting clearly separated advertising space between newspaper articles or television programmes. These meeting places do not always ensure that brands reach their consumers when or where they are at their most receptive. Just because people are in search of information or entertainment does not mean they are after information or entertainment from a particular brand at that specific moment. Think about it: an evening television commercial for breakfast cereal is a long way from the moment of consumption.

In short, the platform offered by traditional media channels is no more than a compromise. Rather than giving brands the opportunity to truly infiltrate people's lives or interact with them directly, traditional media channels keep the two sides at a distance.

Ideally, brands would reach consumers directly without having to involve in-between channels. There are two ways of drawing consumers and brands closer to each other.

BRAND ⟷ CONSUMER

The first is for the brands to go where the people are, to be mobile and to follow in the footsteps of the consumer. The increasing success of home parties, guerrilla tactics and buzz marketing is part of this attempt. Take PIXMAN, for example, a medium whereby promotion staff are equipped with video screens or digital projectors. A so-called 'nomadic' medium, it shows video clips in targeted venues and in specific public places, allowing brands to go where the public is rather than waiting for the public to come to them. Founder Bas Berendsen calls it the first mass medium capable of going after a desired target group. Similarly, guerrilla ads planted in very specific environments have much the same effect since they too have the ability to penetrate places normally inaccessible to brands.

A second way to get up close and personal with consumers is the reverse tactic: for brands to be more inviting and transparent, to encourage consumers to step inside their world. The Internet is the perfect tool for this, allowing people to interact with brands on their own terms. Consumers can retrieve information about a company, its brands and its products whenever it suits them, not the other way around. Experiential marketing is another discipline that brings together companies and consumers. A staged event or experiential platform can expose a brand to the public.

These tactics establish a closer, more intense relationship between people and brands. Brands should not rely on meeting consumers 'in the middle', at an artificially created meeting point. **'Your place or mine?' should be the opening line for a successful relationship between brands and consumers.**

This original promotion for British Airways placed the brand and its message in the midst of potential customers rather than talking to them from a distance (see p. 155).

Exclusivity or going where the competition is not

For any brand, the ultimate fantasy is to have some time alone with consumers without competing messages stealing their attention. Conventional advertising formats are particularly poorly suited to this as they offer only loud and over-crowded places. Commercial breaks on television show an uncontrolled mix of branded messages: an advert about diet yoghurt may be preceded or followed by a message about toilet-cleaning products. Yet brands still crave their intimate, quiet corner, even if it is obtained by buying all the advertising space in and around a programme or, in the ultimate ironic coup, by sponsoring an ad-free transmission. For example, in the USA, the beer brand Miller sponsored an ad-free transmission for the first episode of the drama series *Rescue Me* and Starbucks bought all commercial breaks within highly acclaimed films on four Fridays in a row. In much the same way, companies pay vast sums of money to become exclusive sponsors of big events, leading to an even stronger and purer connection between the brand and the experience sponsored. These are the kind of drastic (financial) measures companies have to take if they want special time alone with their audience.

This shows that the Holy Grail for brands remains an exclusive, uncluttered environment specifically suited to their profile. Yet rather than preventing the competition from infiltrating crowded places, it may be financially (and otherwise) more rewarding to seek out areas that are still untouched. And, once you step off the canvas of conventional media, there are plenty of these areas around. Consider what Meow Mix did when they set up a temporary Kitty restaurant in the heart of New York (see campaign 198, p. 179). It was also the logic behind IKEA's decision to use elevators as a branding space in China (see campaign 139, p. 129). In so doing, IKEA made the strategic decision to go where the competition was not and booked some time alone with the consumer.[2] The search for exclusivity explains the increasing importance given to designing retail environments and staging events. These communication domains allow companies to create environments where they are in full control of the experience.

Brands are continuously on the lookout for places, moments and media where they can enjoy people's devoted and undivided attention. Mercedes-Benz, for example, turned the Ritz Carlton into an exclusive channel for their 'Key to Luxury' campaign. For the duration of their stay in any of the Ritz-Carlton hotels, guests were offered the use of a CLS500 with unlimited mileage, a full tank of petrol each morning and overnight valet parking. According to the Ritz Carlton, dozens of guests decided to buy new Mercedes based on these novel test-drives.[3] Had the car company been forced to share the Ritz Carlton with ten other automobile brands it is unlikely that the same impact would have been achieved.

No matter how desirable this kind of exclusivity is, it is hard to measure its qualitative impact. 'How to put an empirical value on an uncluttered environment?', Mark Austin and Jim Aitchinson ask in *Is Anybody Out There?*. 'Exclusivity is power,' they add.[4] **The less you have to share the attention of consumers with fellow advertisers, the more power you can exert over consumers.**

While exclusivity is a powerful factor in choosing media, there are exceptions to the rule. It can without a doubt be worthwhile for two brands to work hand in hand, either for long-term causes or on a particular occasion, as long as both parties gain from the collaboration, as in the case of Ritz-Carlton and Mercedes. If another brand makes your brand or company look younger, cooler, classier, more contemporary or more competent, any kind of association is beneficial. If you see no added value, you are better off on your own.

It was an unusual and off-the-wall decision by Evian to sponsor the renovation of this lido, but it paid off. The pool became fondly known by everyone as 'The Evian Lido' and the brand reaped the benefits (see p. 53).

Invisibility or moving the brand to the background

In guerrilla warfare, invisibility is a mighty weapon. Whereas traditional warfare is an open, face-to-face confrontation, guerrilla warfare cherishes the art of disguise and surprise. Games of hide-and-seek have also affected the relationship between brands and consumers. And, the intensity and level of the game is continuously rising since both parties are increasingly aware of each others' hiding places and techniques.

Conventional advertising is very bad at hide-and-seek, giving itself away before the game has even begun. It is so visible, so explicit, so identifiable as advertising that consumers easily spot it and tune out. Take television, not only is the commercial nature of the messages overt but the broadcaster's introduction to the commercial break acts like an alarm bell. Viewers know what is coming, so it is easy for them to filter out or zap the adverts away. 'When we put six to eight 30-second commercials back to back, we put up a sign saying "Go away now",' says Peter Chernin, News Corp.'s president and chief operating officer.[5] It is precisely this undisguised visibility, this clear line between content and commerce that makes the traditional television commercial so vulnerable to the growing ad-skipping technology. Since commercials can be separated easily from the content viewers have chosen to watch, they can just as easily be skipped altogether.

Advertising that gets away with it is advertising that does not look or feel like advertising. It is the advertising or communication that blends in seamlessly with real entertainment, real events or real life to the extent that it is not possible to tell what is advertising and what is not. **What smart product placement, cleverly devised guerrilla tactics, branded content and word of mouth all have in common is that they are harder to trace and label as advertising. And, something that is harder to trace is also harder to ignore.** Consumers do not like to 'smell the sell' and that applies specifically to youngsters. When Tylenol helped to fund an indoor skateboarding area in Brooklyn, it decided not to put its logo anywhere. Despite, or perhaps thanks to, the lack of obvious visible branding, skateboarders and the specialist skating magazines spontaneously christened it 'The Tylenol Bowl'. This result is consistent with the findings of a study carried out by the Singapore-based ad agency Red Card. Called *Secret Lives*, it maps out the way youngsters deal with media and brands. One conclusion was that unbranded content works better than branded content.[6] **In other words, while visibility is the mantra in conventional advertising, in an ad-cynic era it proves more effective to be as invisible, as small and as humble as possible. The less pushy and the less dominant the commercial nature of the message, the more chance it has of being digested.** Brands cannot simply force their way into the lives of consumers; they need to act like chameleons and subtly blend in.

Taking the smell out of the sell has little to do with reducing the size of the brand's logo; rather, it is about creating genuine improvements in consumers' lives. Take the Tylenol example. Instead of focusing on how they could ensure that every skater could see the Tylenol brand name, the company was more concerned about improving the lives of skaters. Helping to fund an indoor skating area did just that, and, as a result, the skaters were more than happy to attribute the initiative to Tylenol. **Brands cannot enforce recognition and attribution. They have to earn it.** When brands act as benefactors, recognition or attribution can be assured by a subtle signature or by telling a number of select people who then spread the word. Hewlett-Packard came to the aid of young artists by opening a gallery where they could print and project their work using HP printers and projectors (see campaign 208, p. 187). The gallery was named HYPE Gallery, subtly referring to the brand's name without ever mentioning it overtly. The artistic films that announced the project were inspired by words beginning with 'H' and 'P', resulting in such film titles as *HorsePlay, Hairy Pooches* and *Hedonistic Penguin*. Rather than plastering Hewlett-Packard's name all over the gallery, the company opted for a more indirect and less visible approach. There were no HP logos present in the gallery, except on the technology itself. As it turned out, exit interviews showed that 19 out of 20 artists realized the HP connection to the HYPE project.[7] It is precisely this kind of humbleness that has a much greater effect in the long term.

Unpredictability or catching consumers off guard

The fourth factor driving the communication between brands and consumers is unpredictability. **Genuinely unpredictable uses of media, leading to the 'A-ha!' effect, cut through any level of cynicism.** Today, you have to really push the envelope to reach that point, but it is definitely worth it. When Richard Branson drove a World War II tank through the streets of Manhattan to announce the launch of Virgin Cola, it was a truly unpredictable move. It simply was not something you saw every day and it captured perfectly what Virgin Cola is all about (see campaign 211, p. 191). This form of communication not only catches people when they are in an open and receptive state of mind, but news of it also travels very fast, earning its weight in gold through free publicity and word of mouth.

Conventional advertising lacks unpredictability. It is hard to catch consumers off guard if a message is planted in the middle of a commercial block on television. Our eyes, minds and ears have been trained to spot advertising messages. We have recognized these advertising formats for decades and they have been subject to very little change. They are burdened with a degree of predictability that stands in the way of genuine surprise.

The essence of unpredictability means that you cannot announce yourself beforehand. A surprise party is only successful if the person it is for is unaware that something is happening. The more unexpected the party, the better the effect. The only caveat is relevance: there is not much sense in throwing a surprise party if the recipient would dislike having one.

The hard part is finding an unexpected angle – whether you refer to it as 'under the radar' or the consumer's 'back door' or 'weak spot' – from which to approach people. True unpredictability demands that you are one step ahead, so key elements are agility and mobility. In guerrilla warfare, attacks are swift, sudden and unexpected, to unnerve and confuse the opponent[8]. The more unpredictable a campaign, the more chance it has of gaining people's honest and immediate attention. **Consumers should not be expected to have to fit into categories predefined by the brand. Brands should fit in with the unpredictable behaviour of the consumer.**

Opposite The success of the HYPE Gallery proves that a brand with a humble and generous attitude is more easily and naturally accepted by consumers than one that forces its brand name and message on people (see p. 187).

Left Two men playing football at great heights while attached to a billboard – it is not something you see every day when you are out shopping (see p. 196).

Measuring the value of a medium

For many advertisers, one of the main obstacles preventing them from using alternative communication techniques is the lack of clear data and research on their impact and reach. How do you measure word of mouth? How do you assess the real effect of stunts or wild postings? Leaving conventional media channels is very adventurous but, at the end of the day, companies need to know that they have reached their desired target audience in the best possible way.

This raises the issue of quantity versus quality. In advertising research, the stress has always been on the quantitative dimension: how to reach X number of people. Every television channel, newspaper and magazine can tell you how many people you can reach through their particular medium. If you put an ad in the paper, you will have the figures to show exactly how many people ought to have seen it.

Quality has always come second, partly because it is harder to quantify. There are few figures, for example, to show how many times an ad was ignored, how many people made the effort to read the text, how many people believed what they read, how many people told other people about it, how many people forwarded the message via email. **Counting how many people saw a concert, read a paper or watched a programme is easy. Assessing the true impact of an advert is hard. How do you quantify the credibility, integrity, proximity, unpredictability, uniqueness, exclusivity of a channel or medium?** How do you measure the value of editorial coverage by a newspaper or television channel? Simply adding up the people who have read or seen it will not work because, in terms of impact and credibility, free press coverage greatly out-performs paid-for advertising space. How do you compare the impact of people taking pictures of a stunt with their mobile phones and sending it to their friends with the impact of yet another standard billboard?

To rightly evaluate any medium, you must look at its total value, taking into account both the number of people it reaches (quantity) and its impact (quality). To evaluate the quality of a medium or channel, conventional or not, the four criteria mentioned earlier – proximity, exclusivity, invisibility and unpredictability – can help: how close did it get to the desired target group? How exclusive was the environment in which the message was transmitted? How well did it convey a commercial message without overselling it? How unpredictable, unexpected and surprising was it in approaching the consumer? It is not always easy to quantify these criteria, but a gut feeling and some basic consumer research can shed light on which ideas or channels are winners and which are not.

The amplification effect

A common criticism of alternative advertising techniques is that they only reach a certain number of people directly. While this is quite often the case, there are many ways to amplify the effect so that more people experience it indirectly. The Adidas vertical football stunt (see campaign 219, p. 196) consisted of a single billboard set up for a very short period of time. As a result, only a limited number of people saw the actual stunt. Yet the sight of floating men playing football on top of a billboard ensured that a huge number of people came into contact with it indirectly, through such media as mobile messaging, the Internet, press coverage, and so on. In terms of free publicity alone, the action reaped the astonishing equivalent of $150 million of advertising. The stunt's unexpected and unique nature fuelled its journey through other channels.

The Adidas example shows that an alternative advertising idea can travel far beyond its immediate sphere of influence with little or no effort. **In a world whose universal currency is information, rumours and stories spread in no time. Free publicity and word of mouth can amplify a message or channel that would otherwise have limited reach.** Yet what receives exposure and what does not is not something advertisers can fully control; they can merely encourage talk by launching press releases or spreading messages. Whether an idea finds a place in people's conversations or in the press depends in the first place on its intrinsic qualities – its proximity, relevance, uniqueness and unpredictability.

Conventional advertising also serves as a good way of amplifying alternative advertising. The main difference is that conventional advertising can be controlled by the advertiser and can be part of an integrated communications plan while word of mouth cannot. When organizing an event, sampling or stunt, conventional advertising can be used to announce or create awareness about the action.

Once, conventional advertising was at the heart of any campaign. Anything else was just the cherry on the cake. Now, alternative channels are the cake. They have the ability, power and attraction to run the show, forcing conventional advertising into a subordinate role. In other words, the evolution toward unconventional advertising techniques does not imply the death of traditional formats, it merely changes their hierarchical role in the overall picture.

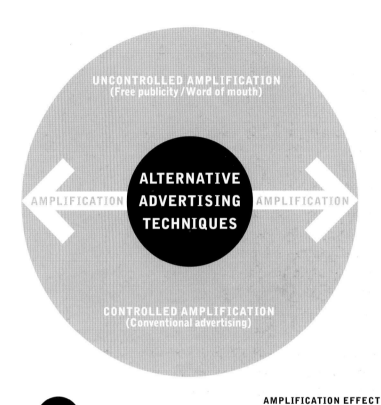

Direct exposure

Indirect exposure

AMPLIFICATION EFFECT
Amplifying alternative advertising techniques means broadening their exposure through free publicity and word of mouth (uncontrolled amplification) or conventional advertising (controlled amplification).

Finding Inspiration

Techniques of alternative advertising

This chapter discusses and presents eight techniques that meet one or more of the four driving forces considered in section one: proximity, exclusivity, invisibility and unpredictability. These eight techniques propose alternative ways to reach people in their most direct environment. They are eight techniques that one way or another have the ability to get under people's skin, to catch them off guard, at a moment, in a place, in a way that they least expect. The eight techniques do not pretend to be exhaustive; the communications landscape is evolving too quickly. Neither do they claim to be mutually exclusive. Good communication campaigns or actions can make use of several techniques at the same time.

Intrusion
Using places or objects as a carrier of the message

Transformation
The physical alteration of something real

Installation
The act of installing something

Illusion
Communication that distorts our perception of what is real and what is not

Infiltration
The use of people to penetrate an area

Sensation
Information conveyed through the senses

Interaction
Any communication in which the consumer is actively involved

Stunt
A difficult, unusual or dangerous feat

Intrusion using places or objects as a carrier of the message

This section is about using new and fresh places, media or surfaces as vehicles for distributing commercial messages. Intrusion occurs whenever commercial messages find new terrain to occupy; this can be within traditional advertising channels, but is especially beyond them. It comprises product placement in movies and television programmes, the attachment of messages to outdoor places and the use of any kind of object as a carrier.

Commercial intrusion, or the use of any imaginable surface for advertising purposes, is a far from recent phenomenon. However, its popularity has increased substantially since the mid-1990s and it now affects public spaces, mobile phones, television and film content – any place or medium where people's attention can be grabbed. Intrusion is a response to the ongoing search for exclusive and new terrain. The ultimate goal is to find territory that is somehow not yet 'tainted' by commerce, that still has a kind of freshness to it. Fresh ground makes it a lot easier to start conversations, as Ken Sacharin points out in *Attention! How to interrupt, yell, whisper, and touch consumers…*: 'It is nearly impossible to command attention in a crowded room. A better strategy would be to find a quieter place to stand – a part of the room that's less noisy and crowded, where even with your sore throat you'd stand at least a chance of getting someone's attention.'[9] In media terms, a quieter place consists of all space that is not yet intruded by commerce.

Although intrusion has a negative ring to it and evokes a sense of 'invading' private territory without consent or permission, it is not necessarily a bad thing. On the contrary, the right message in the right place at the right moment can create a response that is much more favourable than using any conventional media space. **Intrusion permits the advertiser to plant his or her message at a specific place where it has the most relevance for the receiver.** Rather than having your favourite television programme interrupted by a commercial for a product you could not care less about at that moment, would it not be much nicer if you were confronted with the same message at a time and in a place when your mind was on the subject? By intruding into new places in a surprising way advertisers can develop communication that is more relevant, less obnoxious and less irritating for consumers.

However, it is essential that commercial intrusion be treated with absolute care, especially when it concerns the intrusion of non-commercial or public spaces. Drowning the consumer in an arbitrary cloudburst of messages is not a suitable reaction to an ever more ad-sceptic audience surrounded by ever-growing clutter. Yet as long as there is a logical and relevant link between the product or brand message and the terrain that is intruded, surprising and positive brand encounters can result. While true clutter is the result of randomly sticking messages in places without any deliberate or creative logic, there are also ways to make smart and creative use of places.

Using the value of a medium

Clever intrusion happens when the specific characteristics of a surface or space are taken into account and integrated into the message. There is no such thing as virgin territory. Every channel or space possesses four particular characteristics: the purpose or function it fulfils in everyday life (functional value), what it looks like (appearance value), who it connects you with (connection value) and what attention it can generate (attention value). All four characteristics can become part of the message.

Using the functional value of a medium

Most spaces that carry advertising have no other function or purpose. Commercial blocks between television programmes or outdoor billboards, for instance, have no other function than to serve the noble purpose of spreading the sales message. This is quite different from everyday objects that are used as advertising media, such as pizza boxes, coasters, toilets, matches, cinema seats, taxis, plastic dry-cleaning covers, cups, glasses and sugar bags – anything you can think of.

These non-traditional 'media' have a function in everyday life. Pizza boxes keep pizzas hot. Coasters prevent the bar from getting wet. These objects keep performing their functions even when they are being used for advertising purposes.

If an advertiser integrates the functional value of a medium into the message, the medium becomes part of the message. It can provide an injection of humour to the message, which in turn has a favourable effect on its impact. By adapting the message to the medium that distributes it, an advertiser acknowledges his or her intrusive behaviour but is willing to make the intrusion more digestible. It is a form of politeness, you might say, that is welcomed by people. **A campaign that plays with the functional value of a medium results in more entertaining, more amusing and more creative intrusions in our lives.**

1

British television channel E4 made a simple claim: all the best television on one channel. Logically, you would want to dash home for a promise like that. Hasty couriers rushing through town provided the perfect medium to communicate this specific message.

Client **E4**
Agency **Cake**
UK 2001

2

To highlight book sales in Carrefour supermarkets, books being a lesser known product category to most of the store's clients, certain titles were placed next to food products that had a straight connection with the content of the books.

Client **Carrefour**
Agency **Salles Chemistri**
Brazil 2004

3

Supermarkets are by nature very visually busy areas. Nevertheless, this Sonrisal ad covered a surprising and innovative spot: the end of the checkout counter, where consumers often stand waiting and therefore pay more attention to what is around them. Above all, the advertisers made cunning use of the particulars of the location.

Client **Glaxosmithkline**
Agency **Ogilvy Brasil Comunicação**
Brazil 2003

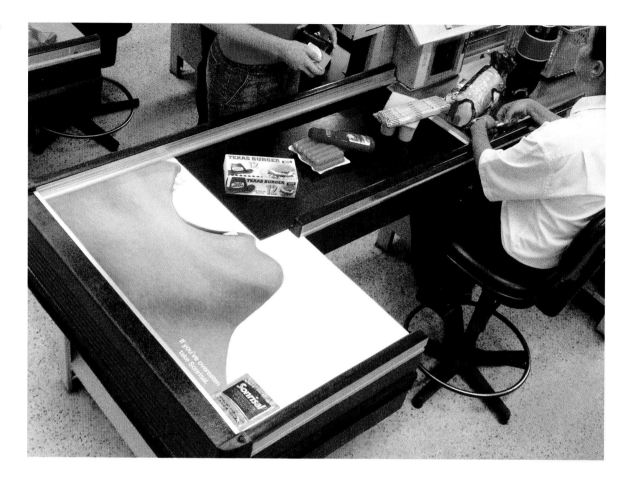

4

On the windows of deserted shops in crowded shopping streets, eBay placed stickers suggesting that the content of the store had moved to eBay. By making use of these empty spaces, eBay attracted the attention of the passing crowd.

Client **eBay**
Agency **mortierbrigade**
Belgium 2005

5

As working out is a very popular pastime among up-market individuals in Singapore, gyms were an ideal place to reach the target audience of *The Economist*. Messages on various pieces of equipment took into account the function of each piece. During the six-week campaign, over 500 new subscriptions were generated.

Client **The Economist**
Agency **Ogilvy & Mather**
Singapore 2004

6

Football referees must have 20/20 vision. As a result, the idea of referees needing glasses is one of the oldest jokes in football. Specsavers, the UK's biggest optical retailer, took advantage of the public's association of referees with good vision. They developed a sponsorship programme that included branding on referee clothing and perimeter boards, eye tests for referees and a training academy for 300 new referees each year. The campaign generated a 22% rise in sales of glasses to men.

Client **Specsavers**
Agency **Mediaedge:CIA**
UK 2002

AMPLIFICATION EFFECT
Highly original, this sponsorship programme generated
£1 million in PR value.

Dog dirt has such strong connotations that it is a fitting carrier for specific kinds of messages.

As part of its merciless and fact-based approach, 'truth' – the ultimate anti-smoking brand – exposed the common properties found in cigarettes and 'dog poop'. The sticks were used in a print campaign and were also planted in real dog poop.

Client **American Legacy Foundation**
Agency **Arnold Worldwide/ Crispin Porter + Bogusky**
USA 2002

Notorious for its brutal honesty in advertising, Hans Brinker Budget Hotel planted small flags in dog dirt to underline its lousy yet cheap offer. These daring actions resulted in worldwide news coverage for the Dutch hotel chain. The flags ran as part of a larger campaign.

Client **Hans Brinker Budget Hotel**
Agency **KesselsKramer**
the Netherlands 1996

9

The campaign for Sony Ericsson's latest photo-messaging mobile phone showed youngsters drooling over the gadget. In line with this central 'drooling' theme, an army of 600 dogs, bearing special branded jackets, was posted across European capitals with the aim of directing people to the website.

Client **Sony Ericsson**
Agency **Strawberry Frog**
the Netherlands 2002

'The richer the media mix, the more surprising, impacting, relevant and downright fun the consumer is likely to find it.'

Scott Goodson, founding creative partner of Strawberry Frog in *Contagious Magazine*

10

One of the most popular performances in an Indian circus is the Well of Death. Daredevils enthral crowds by manoeuvring their motorcycles and cars at breakneck speed round and round the almost vertical walls of a deep pit. Fevicol, a household brand in India that claims to be 'The Ultimate Adhesive', decided to paint the walls with its logo. There is a telling association of the daring behaviour of the stuntmen with the adhesive powers of Fevicol.

Client **Pidilite Industries**
Agency **Ogilvy & Mather Advertising**
India 2003

11

Stuttgart taxi drivers – 70% of whom drive a Mercedes – were made to look as if they secretly dreamt about driving a BMW in this advertisement.

Client **BMW Stuttgart**
Agency **Jung von Matt**
Germany 2003

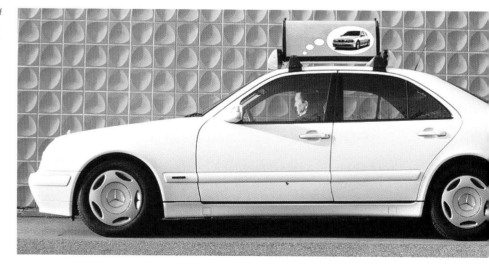

12

A real challenger in the Swedish housing loans market, SBAB fixed their message on their actual product: people's apartments. Speech bubbles were attached to apartments in 20 different locations. The remarkable thing about this campaign is that every word on the signs is absolutely true. The people living in the apartments provided details of their mortgages and the resulting calculations were correct.

Client **SBAB**
Agency **TBWA\Stockholm**
Sweden 2003

13

No better place could have supported the launch of the new Duracell Ultra M3 battery than the chimneys of Battersea Power Station in London. The world's most powerful battery was advertised on the country's most famous icon of power. Initially, it was described as the 'million-pound stunt' by *Campaign* magazine, but in actual fact it only cost £177,000.

Client **Duracell**
Agency **OMD**
UK 2002

14

Ads on manhole covers
playfully position Qantas
as the smartest way to fly
'down under'.

Client **Qantas Airways**
Agency **Publicis Frankfurt**
Germany 2004

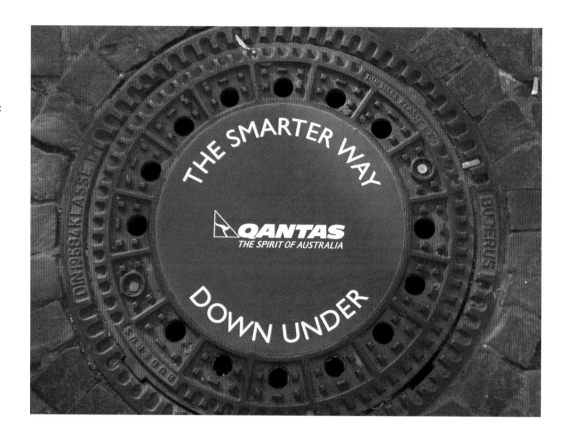

15

Shown here are two of the
media channels that low-cost
airline Hapag-Lloyd Express
used to promote its good-value
pricing. In both cases, the
creative expression made full
use of the functional value of
the medium. 'Why not just fly
to Italy?' was printed on pizza
boxes, while 'Many thanks for
your comments' appeared on
airline sick bags.

Client **Hapag-Lloyd Express**
Agency **Scholz & Friends
Berlin**
Germany 2003

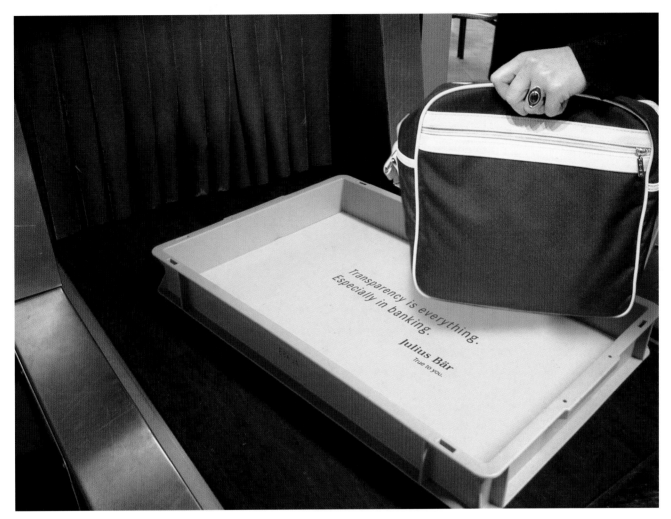

16

For a bank that prides itself on transparency, the security check at airports seemed the perfect spot to advertise. Julius Bär Bank was the first advertiser to secure exclusive use of all the security trays that hold items going through the X-ray machines for a period of one year.

Client **Julius Bär Bank**
Agency **Jung von Matt/ LIMMAT**
Switzerland 2003

Using the appearance value of a medium

Every object or area has an appearance value: a shape, colour and size. Most outdoor billboards are monotonous in their appearance, the only variable being the size of the canvas. But the real-life objects and areas that are used for advertising purposes come in all shapes and formats. By integrating certain external characteristics of a medium into the overall advertising creation, the medium becomes part of the message. Content and space fuse together.

17

For the promotion of Forte 1000 condoms, light-switch covers were placed in local bars, restaurants and stores, turning innocent switches into phallic symbols.

Client **Forte 1000**
Agency **Concept Café**
USA 2004

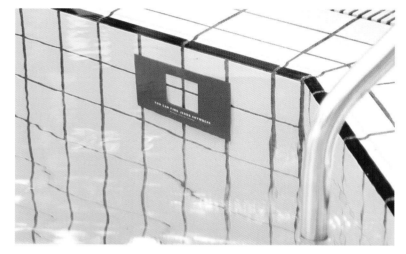

18

Adhesive-backed cards with rectangles cut out of them and carrying the message 'You can find Jesus anywhere' were stuck on a variety of objects in different places. The addition of the card turned these everyday forms into an instantly recognizable religious symbol. Members of the World Revival Prayer Fellowship stuck the cards in the most creative and intriguing locations imaginable to attract more worshippers to the church.

Client **World Revival Prayer Fellowship**
Agency **Batey**
Singapore 2004

19

In this poster campaign for McDonald's, the form and appearance of the medium is fully integrated.

Client **McDonald's**
Agency **Leo Burnett Chicago**
USA 2005

20

A local travel agency integrated the movement of the tides into their creative message on a banner hung on the walls of Hamburg Harbour.

Client **Travel Agency Eppendorf**
Agency **Kolle Rebbe Werbeagentur**
Germany 2003

21

For this campaign denouncing the shortage of drinking water for children in third-world countries, a hand dryer was reconfigured as a thirsty mouth.

Client **World Vision**
Agency **Publicis Frankfurt**
Germany 2004

Client **Amnesty International**
Agency **TBWA\Paris**
France 2004

22 & 23

Strategically hung posters turned ordinary street fencing or gates into ruthless prison bars or deadly instruments of torture.

Client **Amnesty International**
Agency **He Said She Said**
Germany 2004

24

Barriers at the car parks in Singapore's Central Business District proved to be the perfect medium for British Airways to communicate the spacious legroom in World Traveller Plus seats. For the first few months of the campaign all such seats sold out.

Client **British Airways**
Agency **M&C Saatchi**
Singapore 2003

25

Sugar cubes were suitable carriers to promote Nintendo's cube-shaped game console. Free samples were given to high-end, trendy places where youngsters hang out. Sugar sachets were also handed out, carrying the message: 'I'd rather be a cube'.

Client **Nintendo**
Agency **Cake**
UK 2002

A series of street drawings
for K2r, France's top-selling
laundry stain remover, used
existing oil spots and stains
throughout the city as an
integral part of the ads.

Client **K2r**
Agency **TBWA\Paris**
France 2004

FASHION RIO - 7 A 11 DE JULHO

27

A pair of scissors was painted on the asphalt, cleverly integrating existing street markings. The action highlighted a fashion event at the nearby Museum of Modern Art in Rio de Janeiro.

Client **Museum of Modern Art Rio de Janeiro**
Agency **Quê Comunicação**
Brazil 2004

28

South Africa's city of
Pretoria is home to the
famous Jacaranda trees,
which, although they only
blossom once a year, carpet
the streets and avenues with
purple flowers. What better
location to continue paint
manufacturer Dulux's already
famous promise of 'Any colour
you can think of'.

Client **Dulux**
Agency **Lowe Bull**
South Africa 2004

AMPLIFICATION EFFECT
The billboard received
nationwide coverage
in newspapers and
on television.

Using the connection value of a medium

The connection value of a medium refers to its ability to connect with specific groups of people. A record store, for instance, has the ability to connect with music lovers, while a fitness club attracts people who are interested in healthy living or keeping in shape. These places have a very specific function or purpose and are frequented or used by particular groups of people.

Using such objects and places as advertising media allows immediate access to their connection value. The inside of taxis, for example, connects brands with such specific groups as tourists, business people or people who do not own a car or who cannot drive. To reach dog owners, the non-traditional media channels with the highest connection value are dog salons, specialized dog shops, the dog-food aisle in the supermarket, dog-food products, city parks where dogs are walked, sticks in the park, shelters and dog shows. To find the medium with the highest connection value for a product, it is imperative to clearly outline the target group: what they do, where they live, where they go and with what they come into contact.

29

Research showed Teletext Holidays that 29% of the traffic on their site was generated by people within 1 hour of arriving at work and within 2 hours of getting home. Therefore, the company set itself the goal of being the first and last message commuters remembered on the way to and from work. Underground ticket barriers provided the perfect opportunity to realize this ambition. Barriers in 23 London railway and underground stations held the message: 'Don't go anywhere until you have been to Teletext Holidays'. Despite World Cup distractions, results were up 23% on the previous year.

Client **Teletext**
Agency **Manning Gottlieb OMD**
UK 2002

And we like your old clothes. If you don't need it, bring it to us.

Thank you.

30

There is no better time or place to ask people to give away their old clothes than when they are shopping for new ones. Price labels on new clothes became polite reminders about the Red Cross charity people could support.

Client **Red Cross Croatia**
Agency **McCann-Erickson**
Croatia 2004

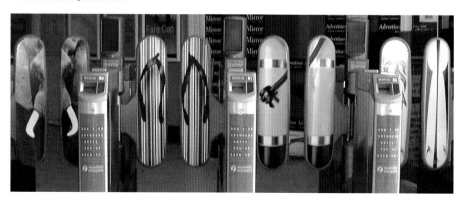

31

Department stores in
Singapore put up stickers
asking people to donate their
old clothes. In the weeks of
the campaign, the number
of clothes delivered to the
Salvation Army tripled.

Client **Salvation Army
Singapore**
Agency **Bates Singapore**
Singapore 2004

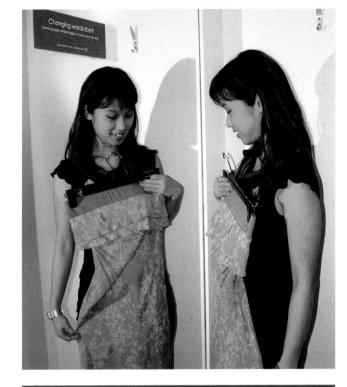

32

Bike saddles were a suitable
medium for outdoor
equipment specialist
Playground to reach their
target group. During a snowy
December, 800 parked bikes
received a special saddle
cover. When the biker later
brushed the snow off he or she
was greeted with the message:

'Hello hard-ass! You ride your
bike when the elements are
against you. That's tough and
we like that, as you know how

to put a steel edge on your
everyday life. If you bike down
to our store without falling
you get a really good offer
on fleece underwear from
Houdini. They make sure your
noble parts also enjoy the hard
life. Since you've been nice all
year you also get a map with
250 other adventures within
biking distance.'

Client **Playground**
Agency **Akestam Holst**
Sweden 2004

33

On 19 January 2003, Canal+ transmitted a historic football match between Real Madrid and Atlético de Madrid. A week prior to the game, the channel announced the coverage in the place where their potential audience was most likely to be assembled: the football stadiums.

As the match was taking place in the Real Madrid stadium (Bernabéu), Canal+ distributed leaflets on the seats of the Atlético de Madrid stadium. The leaflets, which resembled a typical football supporter's scarf, read on one side, 'No way I'm going to Bernabéu' and, on the other, 'I'd rather watch it on Canal+'. By dialling the phone number provided supporters could subscribe to Canal+. Of the phone calls received the following week, 22% were from people who had picked up the leaflet in the stadium.

Client **Canal+**
Agency **Remo D6**
Spain 2003

AMPLIFICATION EFFECT
A very well-known Spanish television presenter, an Atlético supporter, showed the leaflet during his programme.

34
Murals paying tribute to top
Argentinian football players
were painted near *Potreros*,
a slang term for places where
people hang out to play
football, as part of a Nike
campaign. It is hard to imagine
a place that connects better
with young football lovers.

Client **Nike**
Agency **BBDO Argentina**
Argentina 2004

Using the attention value of a medium

The extent to which a medium is able to grab people's attention is one of its main features. When looking for a suitable non-traditional carrier for a message, remember that some places or objects simply have a higher attention value than others. It can be as a result of their size, their location or their specific qualities. It makes sense that places covered with ads have a lower attention value than virgin territory. The question is: at what point in time or in what place do you have the most chance of getting people's attention? One answer is in places where people have nothing to focus their attention on and are, therefore, more open to messages. This means at bus stops, train stations, launderettes, waiting rooms at doctors or dentists, but there are far more innovative places available that have high attention values.

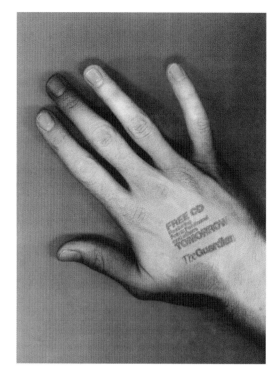

36 & 37

Since we are forced to look at them all the time, our own hands or arms serve as good places to write down things we do not want to forget. These two campaigns made clever use of the attention value of these areas.

London-based national newspaper *The Guardian* used people's hands to promote one of their free CDs. A promotional team stamped the hands of gig goers at over 60 major live-music venues across the UK on the Friday evening prior to the promotion. The following morning, the stamp reminded music lovers that *The Guardian* carried a free CD that day.

Client **The Guardian**
Agency **ClaydonHeeley JonesMason**
UK 2001

35

An attractive girl's bottom is a guaranteed source of attention, which was undoubtedly why *FHM*, the popular men's magazine, tattooed 20 girls on UK beaches with the slogan 'FHM approved!'.

Client **FHM**
Agency **Cunning**
UK 2003

To promote a tattoo parlour, a stamp was designed that integrated the parlour's logo and phone number into a popular Celtic-style tattoo. The area's nightclubs stamped the hands of their guests on entry, so the tattoo parlour stamp was supplied to the trendiest venues. By the end of the evening the target audience knew where to go for a real tattoo.

Client **Kevin's Kustom Tattoos**
Agency **The Jupiter Drawing Room**
South Africa 2004

 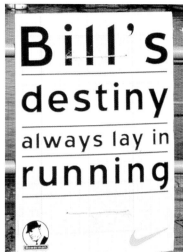  

39

A national newspaper's front page is a very coveted space for advertisers due to its high attention value. This ad brilliantly infiltrated the newspaper's title, perfectly illustrating the Smart Car as one of the smallest cars in the world, which can park almost anywhere.

Client **DaimlerChrysler**
Agency **Springer & Jacoby**
Germany 2003

38

While running a marathon participants are very aware of their surroundings, which is why Nike decided to tell the story of the Two Oceans Marathon's founder, Bill Bowerman, through a series of posters along the 56km route. In a questionnaire completed after the race, many competitors not only recalled the Bowerman story but also claimed they looked forward to reading the story along the way.

Client **Nike**
Agency **The Jupiter Drawing Room**
South Africa 2002

Other channels, other owners

Most traditional media channels are in the hands of media conglomerates, ranging from local players to multinational networks. They offer advertisers an audience in exchange for a financial contribution. When it comes to using alternative channels and carriers, however, different types of owners are involved. Four specific channels and owners are:
- **media or spaces that advertisers own themselves**
- **media or spaces that belong to the public domain**
- **media or spaces occupied by competitors or other advertisers**
- **media or spaces created by advertisers out of nothing, hence having no owners.**

Privately owned media

The media that are most often underestimated as branding tools are those already owned by advertisers, from employee cars to company buildings, from product packaging to stationery and from freebies to company uniforms. These carriers are traditionally subject to severe corporate guidelines, but they offer far greater opportunities than most companies realize. Take packaging, for instance, which has to bear so much practical information – legal requirements, list of ingredients – that there is barely any space for anything else. Packaging design can be one of the most heavily debated issues in a company, yet debates tend to centre on achieving the right colour, the right font or, more generally, the right brand 'style'. The space available on packaging is very rarely used as a proper communication medium, a way to start conversations with consumers and convey what the brand is about.

Aside from the fact that they are completely free and exclusive, privately owned spaces have other specific strengths. First, they are often very close to the company product or service and, as a result, can reach consumers at the moment and place of consumption. Food and beverage packaging, bank terminals and flight attendants' uniforms are able to reach existing customers as they experience the company product or service. Second, privately owned media are often regular meeting points with consumers: a mobile operator or power supplier has a monthly appointment with their clients by means of an invoice. Making full use of this carrier enables a brand to develop a regular relationship with its customers. How often do you find yourself staring at the bottle of water on the dinner table or the jar of coffee in the cupboard? With a little imagination, each of these silent moments could be turned into an inspiring contact with the brand.

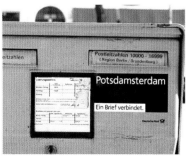

40
By stencilling its postboxes with wordplay, the German post service evoked the sensation that letters create connections across countries and continents.

Client **Deutsche Post**
Agency **Jung von Matt**
Germany 2003

AMPLIFICATION EFFECT
Innocent Drinks teamed up
with EAT cafés, where the
drinks were sold and postcards
distributed to encourage people
to knit. In total, about 25,000
hats were knitted.

41

Innocent Drinks is famous for
writing funny information on
the labels of their smoothies.
This strategy was originally
born out of necessity, since the
start-up company had no
budget for fancy advertising
and decided to make maximum
use of the 3-x-3cm labels on
the small bottles. It quickly
proved the ideal way to start
a dialogue with the people who
drank their smoothies.

The company went one step
further when it asked grannies
around the country to knit
mini bobble hats to put on the
smoothies. For each hat knitted,
a financial contribution went
straight to the charities
supporting day centres, thereby
keeping the old ladies warm
and happy.

Advertiser **Innocent Drinks/EAT**
UK 2005

42

Figuring that men need all the
help they can get to socialize
comfortably with women,
Molson started a campaign
that repackaged the Canadian
beer with 'twin labels'. The
label on the front of the bottle
featured the traditional
Molson logo, while a second
label on the back displayed
lustful, candid, funny, corny,
provocative and conversation-
provoking statements.
Beginning with 84 messages,
they eventually ran over 230
variations. After the
campaign, Molson sales were
up 48% and it became the
fastest growing major import
in the United States.

Client **Molson USA**
Agency **Crispin Porter +
Bogusky**
USA 2003

AMPLIFICATION EFFECT
Molson Twin Label Technology,
as it came to be known, was
also promoted in print, on
television and through a
specially dedicated website
(www.molsontwinlabel.com),
with the tagline: 'Let your
Molson do the talking'.

'Christian de Neuvillette
had his Cyrano de
Bergerac, and now
thousands of tongue-
tied barflies will have
Molson Canadian beer
labels to help them
captivate the object(s)
of their desire.'

USA Today

Publicly owned media

This category includes all media that are public property and fall under the responsibility of a local or national authority: pavements, streets, bins, poles, trees, parks, walls of houses and buildings. Public territory was traditionally the terrain of graffiti artists, who challenged the ownership of council and corporation space, turning public space into a permanent, real-life art gallery and a tool for personal expression. Over the decades, the differences in styles and materials have grown: oil or acrylic paint, airbrush, oil-based chalk, stencils, posters and stickers, to name a few. This has lead to such terms as 'post-graffiti', 'neo-graffiti' or, more generally, 'street art', which refer to the work of train-writers, paste-up artists, poetic doodlers, muralists and protest artists.

With the rising popularity of graffiti art, guerrilla advertising companies have adopted these techniques, sending out armies of people to colonize public spaces for branding purposes. Originally used to promote club nights, bands and record labels, these practices have now been adopted by major companies and brands with the single motivation of improving their street credibility. In their pursuit of respect from youngsters, corporate organizations use street language to win them over, very aware that conventional advertising cannot accomplish this.

In terms of reach, public spaces offer great advantages. Strategic locations, such as shopping streets or centrally located squares, are accessed by a large number of people. On the other hand, by choosing the right public locations, advertisers can target particular groups very effectively. In response to the rising visual pollution of public property, city councils have developed more stringent regulations. However, although in most countries, for instance, it is forbidden to use pavements for advertising purposes, washable chalk or other degradable substances offer a way around this potential offence.

43

Chalk drawings in Prague make no mistake about the cruelties exposed at the city's Museum of Torture.

Client **Museum of Torture Prague**
Agency **Leo Burnett Czech Republic**
The Czech Republic 2003

44

Bottled-water supplier Evian sponsored the repair of a run-down public pool in the London borough of Brixton. In exchange, Evian was allowed to tile its brand name on the bottom of the pool. Quickly, the spot was christened the 'Evian Lido'. As an added bonus, the message was hard to miss for passengers flying in and out of nearby Heathrow Airport.

Client **Evian**
Agency **Cake**
UK 2001

45

What goes down the drain goes into the sea. To raise awareness about the consequences of this, creatures that swim and live in the sea took on a life of their own on the streets of Auckland. The campaign was timed to coincide with an important event, when more people than ever were out and about. Giant street paintings took shape around drains in the densest foot-traffic locations.

Client **Auckland Regional Council**
Agency **Saatchi & Saatchi**
New Zealand 2000

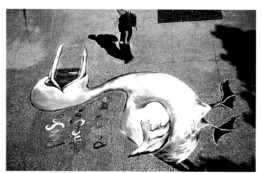

46

In search of additional exposure for their acclaimed 'Odyssey' television commercial, Levi's projected the film onto large eye-catching buildings across Europe. Based on such criteria as suitability for projection and proximity to youth culture, locations in 13 European cities, from Rome to Brussels, were chosen.

Client **Levi's**
Agency **Diabolical Liberties/Starcom Motive**
2002

AMPLIFICATION EFFECT
The activity was further promoted by the distribution of magnets, which were attached to street furniture and given out in bars and cafés.

Lisbon

Rome

Paris

London

Brussels

Berlin

47

Cell C, the young challenger brand in the South African telecommunications sector, commissioned local artists to express their positive reflections on urban life. The completed works of art were photographed, enlarged and placed on the sides of buildings in various locations throughout Johannesburg. Rather than using the Cell C logo, the artists incorporated Cell C's brand iconography. The space covered amounted to the equivalent of 329 rugby fields, thus turning the heart of Johannesburg's Central Business District into a massive outdoor art gallery.

Client **Cell C**
Agency **Network BBDO**
South Africa 2003

48

Statistics showed that only 27% of Minnesotans achieved the recommended levels of daily activity. Blue Cross Blue Shield of Minnesota was determined to increase the percentage. Getting people into the gym was not the answer. What they needed to do was change the community's mindset. The brand 'do' was created as a friendly reminder that there are hidden opportunities to do something healthy almost every moment of the day.

Client **Blue Cross Blue Shield**
Agency **Crispin Porter + Bogusky**
USA 2002

Don't let the
machines win.
Take the stairs.

Groove your body for 10 minutes 3 times a day

do.

FINISH do.

START do.

In case of fire take the stairs.
In case of boredom take the
stairs. In case of holiday
overeating take the stairs.
In case of high blood pressure
take the stairs. In case of big
lunch take the stairs. In case of
stress take the stairs. In case of
fudge sundae take the stairs.

Groove your body for 10 minutes 3 times a day.

do.

49

Stencilling on the ground in front of the Red Cross centre in Singapore acted as a rallying call to action. Singaporeans were encouraged to stop being passive bystanders and to learn First Aid.

Client **Starhub**
Agency **Batey**
Singapore 2004

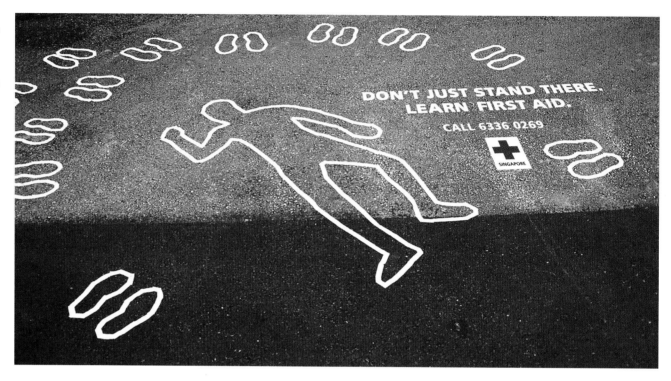

50

In and around cinemas in several Spanish cities, the foyers, cafés, seats, walls, windows and toilets were 'wallpapered' with almost 4.5 million green post-it notes. All of them encouraged consumers to request information about Amena Family Plan, a new telephone tariff.

Client **Amena**
Agency **Starcom Worldwide**
Spain 2003

"Double Drop"

Nobody understands young people better. MTV

51
To show that 'nobody
understands young people
better', MTV placed posters
next to existing graffiti,
translating the words into
an understandable typeface
for everyone.

Client **MTV**
Agency **Age Comunicação**
Brazil 2004

Media occupied by competitors or other advertisers

Most advertisers search for exclusivity in an uncluttered environment, preferring to be as far away as possible from other advertisers. There are, however, various reasons why one brand would be interested in using another brand's advertising space, whether for friendly or hostile motives.

Some of the following campaigns consider what happens if two parties have complementary profiles and a link between them proves beneficial. In such a case, an agreement is reached whereby one advertiser is allowed to use a suitable space on another's campaign, or one party is permitted to make clever comments on another's advertising. Adding an extra element to existing advertising can create altogether new meanings.

Other campaigns shown here focus on hostile relationships, when one party would not so much 'share' as 'hijack' space from the other. Anti-branding and anti-advertising groups, for instance, protest against commerce's invasion of public space by hijacking advertising space. Protest messages in the form of stickers or graffiti on billboards comment on the false and corrupt nature of advertising. Advertising space is also hijacked by people looking for an outlet for their frustration or anger toward a corporation.

52
Collaboration between Mercedes-Benz and Kinder Surprise producer Ferrero resulted in 252,000 eggs filled with model construction kits for a Mercedes E-Class. On the day of the launch, the eggs were given away at Mercedes-Benz dealers.

Client **DaimlerChrysler**
Agency **Springer & Jacoby**
Germany 2003

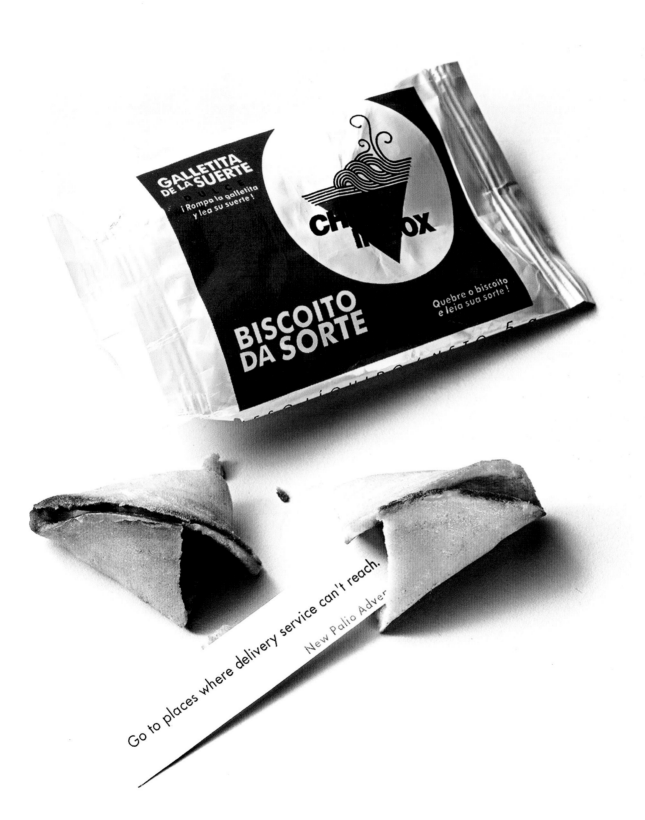

53

Fiat developed a partnership with a chain of Chinese take-aways for the launch of its adventurous Palio model. Through the agreement, Fiat used the fortune cookies that went out with people's orders to promote the car. This partnership, which was part of an integrated campaign, helped to exceed by 35% the target number of test-drives.

Client **Fiat**
Agency **Leo Burnett Brazil**
Brazil 2004

54

During the 2004 electoral campaign in Quebec, candidate posters covered the province. It happened that each of the three party leaders was shown wearing a suit. Clothing brand Henri Vézina grabbed the opportunity to make use of the electoral posters by putting up their own posters showing the candidates' 'other half'.

Client **Henri Vézina**
Agency **BOS**
Canada 2004

AMPLIFICATION EFFECT
The three posters were the subject of a newspaper campaign on three consecutive full pages.

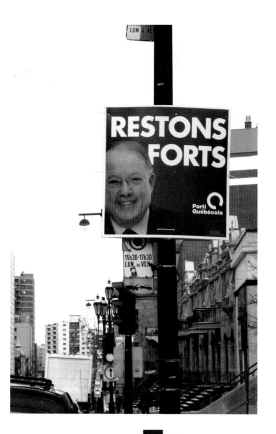

55

A mild form of hijacking occurred with this Nicorette billboard campaign, which was particularly special due to its superb timing. It was launched on 14 February 2003, the very day that tobacco advertising on billboards was banned in the UK. Nicorette pasted over all 800 sites carrying cigarette advertising with a Marlboro spoof billboard entitled 'Welcome to Nicorette Country'.

Client **Pharmacia**
Agency **OMD**
UK 2003

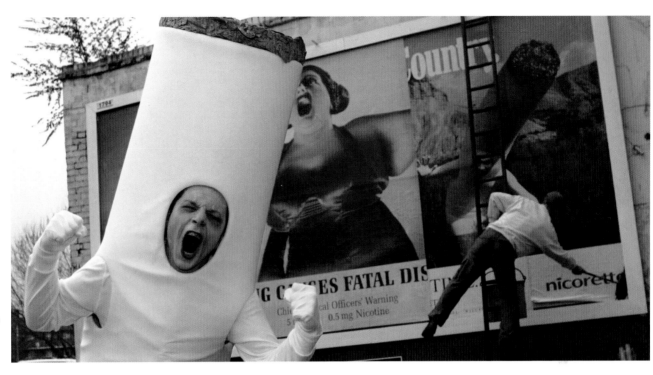

AMPLIFICATION EFFECT
The action drew more attention by the presence of the Craving Man, the star of the Nicorette campaign, which resulted in additional media coverage and visibility.

56

When the battery in his first-generation iPod failed in October 2003 after only 18 months, the young Casey Neistat was dismayed to learn that Apple did not, at the time, offer a replacement battery. His only option was to purchase a new iPod. Casey was unaware of this policy prior to his inquiry and after some discussion with his brother, Van, the Neistat Brothers took it upon themselves to better inform consumers. Casey spray-painted dozens of Apple's pretty pastel iPod posters in and around Manhattan with the warning: 'iPod's Unreplaceable Battery Lasts Only 18 Months'.

Authors **Casey and Van Neistat**
USA 2003

AMPLIFICATION EFFECT
Van filmed his brother defacing the posters and turned it into a 3-minute film, called 'iPod's Dirty Secret', ironically produced on Apple hardware using iMovie software. The film was posted online and in just 6 weeks it had been downloaded over a million times. The controversy surrounding the film, with a production cost of roughly $40, was covered globally by over 130 sources. A few days after their film had gone online, but not necessarily in response to it, Apple began offering a battery replacement programme.

57

South Africa's Standard Bank wanted to demonstrate to a trendy audience what they would be able to buy with an Achiever account. Fake credit card slips and signed cheques were stuck onto existing magazine adverts for such up-market, aspirational brands as Guess, Hugo Boss and Timberland. To maximize association with these brands, the cheques and slips were made out to the particular brand.

Client **Standard Bank of South Africa**
Agency **TBWA\Hunt Lascaris**
South Africa 2003

Created media

If it proves too hard to find an existing medium, perhaps it would be easier to create one yourself. You just need to figure out what would help to carry the message and to gain access to the target audience. For instance, at a festival or gathering, sponsors vie to come up with the hottest, most talked about and most visible gadget to give out. At a music festival, for example, these 'created media' can range from slippers to lanyards to tents. Generally, the funniest, most surprising but also most relevant and user-friendly objects tend to score the highest.

When an audience is not so readily assembled, there are still plenty of objects that can serve as a medium and there is no limit to what can be done. Created media come with the huge benefit that there are no intermediaries. Only the cost of creating and distributing the medium needs to be financed.

58

To underline Illy's strong connection with art and creative expression, the famous Italian coffee brand decided to use sets of espresso cups and saucers as a medium. Hence, the infamous Illy collections were born. Individual artists use their ingenuity and imagination to transform these everyday items into objects of beauty that greatly enrich the coffee-drinking experience.

Some of the most important representatives of the international art community, as well as a number of emerging young talents, have contributed to the project, from Robert Rauschenberg to Jeff Koons, from Joseph Kosuth to James Rosenquist. Since the project's inception in 1992, over fifty artists have created Illy collections. Illy continues to support their work in a variety of ways.

Advertiser **Illy**
Worldwide, from 1992

59

Placed in bars and nightclubs, these candles demonstrated how easily smokers' lives can go up in smoke.

Client **Singapore Cancer Society**
Agency **M&C Saatchi Singapore**
Singapore 2004

60

To inform people about the arrival of the perilous Afghan winter and its disastrous consequences for Afghan children, over 5,000 leaves peppered the ground in central London at bus stops, tube stations and on pavements. The leaves urged the public to act promptly and donate money to Unicef. Being biodegradable, the leaves avoided any problems of litter.

Client **Unicef**
Agency **TEQUILA\London**
UK 2003

AMPLIFICATION EFFECT
Costing less than £500 to execute, generating over £180,000 of free editorial coverage and raising over £1.9 million for Afghan refugees, this campaign is considered among the most cost-effective single campaigns in the history of fundraising.

61

Golfers interviewed in early 2004 predicted that the forthcoming Ryder Cup was going to be the most competitive ever. This time it was going to be war. Branded, camouflaged golf balls played on this idea of a battleground to promote UK newspaper *The Guardian*'s 68-page Ryder Cup special. In total 50,000 balls were planted in hoppers on driving ranges and on counters at pro shops across the country – spot on targeting for the desired audience. Paper sales increased by 47,000, 2,000 copies over target, and there were 18,000 additional visits to *The Guardian* website.

Client **The Guardian**
Agency **ClaydonHeeley**
JonesMason
UK 2004

62

To highlight the growing number of street children being kidnapped, Unicef randomly placed teddy bears in Copenhagen's public spaces, such as pavements, trains and train stations.

Client **Unicef**
Agency **Young & Rubicam Copenhagen**
Denmark 2003

63

In the Sydney Dogs Home, every dog that cannot be re-housed is killed. Sticks were dropped in parks and public walking areas and used as a direct mailing to raise awareness and convince people to get a dog. As a result, instead of 70% of the dogs being put to sleep forever, the same percentage now sleep happily somewhere else. The home also raised $30,000 and attracted a huge amount of media coverage and new sponsors.

Client **Sydney Dogs Home**
Agency **M&C Saatchi**
Australia 2003

64

While waiting for their luggage to appear on the carousel, airline passengers saw how even the most fragile items were handled with care by Virgin Atlantic.

Client **Virgin Atlantic**
Agency **Network BBDO**
South Africa 1999

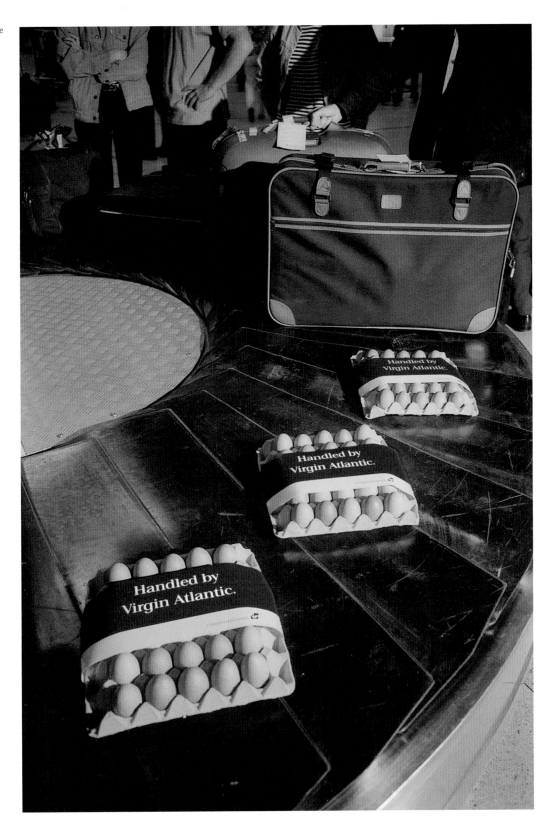

Transformation the physical alteration of something real

When Christo and Jeanne-Claude wrapped the Berlin Reichstag in sheets, the city's main political building became the centre of attention and attracted huge crowds, both from Berlin and other areas. Berliners were mesmerized by the piece of art because before Christo had taken on the famous landmark, the building had become 'wallpaper' for the city's inhabitants. The famous wallpaper effect refers to the diminution of our response when we are repeatedly exposed to the same stimulus. It not only happens with grey, everyday things, but also with amazing and awesome things. Famous landmarks, which people travel continents to see, end up becoming a part of our daily background if we happen to live or work next to them. Only when a transformation occurs, for example, when an artist covers up a landmark, do people feel a startling sense of rediscovery. If a wallpaper is transformed, it again demands attention and comes to the foreground. If a building in your street is painted or the façade is reconstructed, you suddenly notice that the building is there. **Transformation is a fantastic way to grab attention.** As one commentator noted on the Berlin Reichstag: 'The wrapping of the Reichstag will remind us of the limits of our perceptions and how uncertain our knowledge is…. What remains is the form under soft, draping material, the transformed, alienated contours. Christo's drawings can only hint at what we will really see. But it will be new and it will be transient.' It is exactly this effect that transformation as a communication technique searches for. **It is about making the wallpaper visible again and creating a fresh appearance.**

Transformation is reality with a twist. Transformation takes objects and elements that surround us in our everyday life as tools for communication. Whether it is a cigarette lighter, a pen, a shoe, a street lamp, a car, a shopping bag, a square or a building, an amazing number of ordinary things pass through our hands or cross our daily path. Most of these objects have become wallpaper. Transformation alters one or more of the objects' characteristics, be it the colour, shape, size or matter. It could also mean taking away or adding a substantial element, thereby transforming it into something slightly different.

The impact of this technique is derived mainly from the fact that it builds on the existing relationships we have with objects or places in our environment. So a transformation of familiar sights immediately catches our attention. It is seeing your partner after he or she just had a radically different haircut.

While traditional outdoor advertising media are artificially imposed on the urban landscape, having no functional use whatsoever, transformation takes the real world as a starting point and occurs at places and moments we least expect it. To start using this technique, you need to stop looking at the world as a given, but rather as a source of inspiration. Reality is nothing more than a first draft. It has endless potential for transformation, with every object screaming to be twisted, enlarged, coloured, distorted and changed. **Transformation requires that we step out of the rigid framework of traditional advertising and apply creative energy on the world around us.** Transformation can result in surprise and discomfort. Both occur because of the sudden change in something familiar. In the case of the lung-shaped ashtray (campaign 71, p. 78), some people were upset when an ordinary ashtray suddenly became a reminder of the effects of their smoking habit.

Good transformations break through people's mental filters in a surprising and enjoyable way. If done without a smile, it turns very quickly into an aggressive violation of people's environments and has a bad effect. Jeff Goodby of American advertising agency Goodby, Silverstein & Partners said that advertising was an unavoidable part of the environment. He claimed that advertising should be 'a welcome and respected part of what we all have to walk through every day'.[10] Transformation should achieve exactly that: it should cheer up our day, add a sparkle to the grey, monotonous landscape in which we find ourselves. Transformation can take place in eight areas:

- size
- colour
- shape
- matter
- location
- addition
- removal
- replacement

Transformation of size

65

To prove that anyone who flies Hapag-Lloyd Express (HLX) can treat themselves to much more shopping, people with oversized bags were sent to shopping centres and airports. The bags were printed with the words: 'Save on your flight. Not on your shopping.'

Client **Hapag-Lloyd Express**
Agency **Scholz & Friends Berlin**
Germany 2003

66

Objects were scaled to exactly
10 times their usual size to
visualize the capability of the
new Olympus 10x Optical
Zoom. They were then placed
in their usual situations.

Client **Olympus**
Agency **Saatchi & Saatchi**
Australia 2004

67

Enlarged everyday objects
reinforced the message on
these billboards for Mini.

Client **Mini**
Agency **Crispin Porter +
Bogusky**
USA 2003

Transformation of colour

68

This 54-floor tower, the most visible symbol in Tokyo's coolest neighbourhood, was illuminated from the inside by green lights in a very special way. The light danced in perfect synchronization with FM Station J-Wave live on air, turning the building into a real-time sound indicator.

Surrounding bars and restaurants all tuned into J-Wave, but the action also made the station hugely popular among twenty to thirty year olds and won it a number one in the audience rating.

Client **J-Wave**
Agency **Dentsu**
Japan 2004

AMPLIFICATION EFFECT
Signs were installed to direct people's view to the 'Singing Tower'. A week after the event, a poster and newspaper campaign highlighted the spectacle.

Transformation of shape

69

This eye-catching transformation conveys how hot the Nissan Maxima is. Such everyday street furniture as rubbish bins, parking meters and street lights were made to seem as if they had melted in the extreme heat. Recessed in a prop wall opposite the pieces of bent steel was the supposed cause of the damage: a Nissan Maxima. The advert appeared in a new location every four days in strategic places in New York and Los Angeles.

Client **Nissan**
Agency **True**
USA 2004

70

The handles on shopping trolleys were bent to offer even the most corpulent people enough 'belly-room'. If your stomach did actually fit in the curve, though, you were seriously encouraged to think about Kellogg's Special K: 'It's about time. Kellogg's Special K – 99% fat-free.'

Client **Kellogg Company**
Agency **Leo Burnett GmbH**
Germany 2003

71

What better time to remind smokers of the hazardous effects of their habit than during the act of smoking? Through a simple yet clever transformation, the ashtray became an in-the-face, on-the-spot reminder of the disastrous consequences smoking has on the lungs.

Ashtrays were distributed on a small scale in pubs, but although they touched raw nerves – some smokers found them too confrontational and smashed them – they were never mass-produced.

Client **Singapore Cancer Society**
Agency **DY&R Wunderman**
Singapore 2002

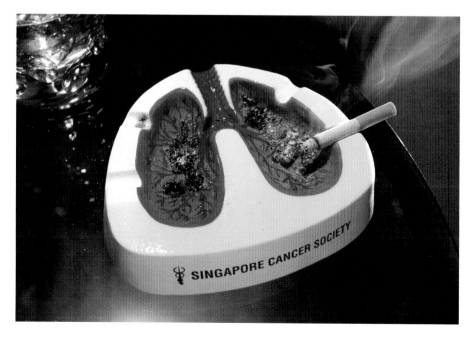

Transformation of matter

72

Few cars today are so cool that they turn heads in the street. To promote the fact that air conditioning comes as standard in the Volkswagen Polo Twist, a life-size replica of the car was sculpted from ice and 'parked' on a busy London street.

The sculpture was made from 9.5 tons of ice imported from Canada. The Ice Box, a company specializing in ice carving, took around 350 hours to create the Polo, which was hand carved by three sculptors in a freezer at -10°C. The final carving weighed approximately 8.5 tons and was transported in 100 individually wrapped sections by freezer freight. Once installed, the car took twelve hours to melt.

Client **Volkswagen**
Agency **DDB London**
UK 2004

AMPLIFICATION EFFECT
The ice car was in fact used in a print advertising campaign. But, before the campaign had broken, well over 11 million people had seen the ice car and knew about the air conditioning due to the PR drive. A direct mail was also sent out, consisting of an ice tray that made Polo-shaped ice.

73

It could have been a scene from the Bible, but this fountain was merely encouraging people to watch the blood-drenched movie *Scream* on New Zealand television channel TV3.

Client **TV3**
Agency **Colenso BBDO**
New Zealand 2000

74

Delegates at the International Whaling Conference in Berlin washed their hands in blood after taps at the conference were secretly fitted with blood tablets. A sign on the mirror reminded people that those who voted for whaling had blood on their hands.

Client **International Fund for Animal Welfare**
Agency **Springer & Jacoby Media**
Germany 2004

IN SOME THIRD WORLD COUNTRIES, THIS IS THE ONLY WATER AVAILABLE.

75 & 76

Two campaigns, one transformation. Clean water was replaced with foul, dirty water to give people an idea of the drinking water available to people in developing countries. In both cases, cups were used as a recruitment tool for new members as contact details were printed on them.

Client **AquAid**
Agency **Harrison Troughton Wunderman**
UK 2003

Client **Unicef**
Agency **Leo Burnett GmbH**
Germany 2004

DRINKING WATER
FOR 1.1 BILLION PEOPLE

Transformation of location

77

To illustrate the added boost
new Adidas A3 basketball
shoes give, rubbish bins in
the streets of Paris were
hung several metres off the
ground at the height of
basketball rims.

Client **Adidas**
Agency **TBWA\Paris**
France 2004

78

To communicate that Virgin Atlantic offers extra legroom in Upper Class, a urinal was installed ridiculously higher than normal in the men's toilets of a national gym chain.

Client **Virgin Atlantic**
Agency **Network BBDO**
South Africa 2003

79

The most suitable environment
in which to advertise the new,
advanced Nike Shox XT7
footwear was on the university
athletics tracks where young
athletes train daily. Prior to
the most important university
athletics meeting of the season,
tracks were subtly transformed.
On the starting grid of the
200m race, the number 8 was
moved from its regular position
further back along the track
and the Nike logo and pay-off
line were stencilled below it.
This transformation conveyed
the message that Nike Shox
make you run faster.

Client **Nike**
Agency **The Jupiter
Drawing Room**
South Africa 2002

Transformation by addition

80

The addition of a single mirror, in the elevators in a shopping mall specializing in computer equipment, illustrated the perfect quality delivered by Hewlett-Packard's Photosmart Printer.

Client **Hewlett-Packard**
Agency **Saatchi & Saatchi**
Singapore 2003

81

In public baby-changing rooms, extra drawings transformed an informative sign into an advertising story.

Client **Procter & Gamble**
Agency **Saatchi & Saatchi**
USA 2004

82

Schöner Wohnen, Germany's biggest and most famous interior-design magazine, promoted a special edition on lighting by adding a touch of style to the street lights in front of Hamburg's Music Hall.

Client **Schöner Wohnen**
Agency **Kolle Rebbe Werbeagentur**
Germany 2000

83

Adding blur and a Nike swoosh to disabled parking signs in the car parks at shopping malls gave the signs a totally different meaning. This transformation was carried out before and during visits from the South African Paralympic Team.

Client **Nike**
Agency **The Jupiter Drawing Room**
South Africa 2001

Transformation by removal

84

Shop mannequins were turned into landmine victims by the removal of one of their legs. A banner revealed the reason behind the transformation: World Landmine Day. The theme was continued inside the shop, where people could buy single children's socks, the proceeds from which went straight to the charity.

Client **Adopt-A-Minefield**
Agency **Saatchi & Saatchi**
South Africa 2002

85 & 86

Both these campaigns used red ballpoints, with their ink removed, as a striking reminder of the situation in the blood banks of both countries. In Singapore, the ballpoints were sent as a direct mailing, while the South African pens were distributed to students on university campuses.

Client **South African National Blood Transfusion Services**
Agency **Saatchi & Saatchi**
South Africa 2002

Client **Red Cross Singapore**
Agency **Ad Planet Group**
Singapore 2003

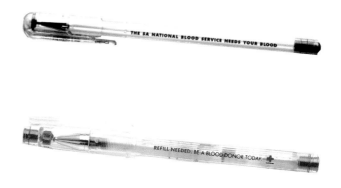

87
To demonstrate Toyota Prius's revolutionary low levels of emissions, posters were erected on very dirty brick walls, framing a small section of the wall that had been thoroughly cleaned.

Client **Toyota Motor Corporation**
Agency **Saatchi & Saatchi**
Australia 2004

88
Why stick paper to walls if you have a product that can create any message you want directly on a wall's surface? The high-pressure cleaner by Bosch removed all dirt except some in the form of letters on exterior walls near shopping centres, leaving behind first-class posters.

Client **Camille Gergen**
Agency **Jung von Matt 1:1**
Germany 2004

Transformation by replacement

89

To make their driving game,
The Getaway, look as real
as possible, PlayStation
accurately re-created digitally
20 square miles of central
London, from the roads,
buildings, shops and cafés to
the traffic lights and zebra
crossings. Tapping into this
fact for the game's launch,
PlayStation sent out a direct
mail containing a London A to
Z map with a twist: names of
streets, parks and landmarks
were changed into *The Getaway*
lingo. *The Getaway* became the
biggest-selling PlayStation title
and the mail pack became a
collector's item.

Client **PlayStation**
Agency **ClaydonHeeley**
JonesMason
UK 2002

AMPLIFICATION EFFECT
PlayStation were so pleased
with the mail pack that they
developed it into press and
trackside posters.

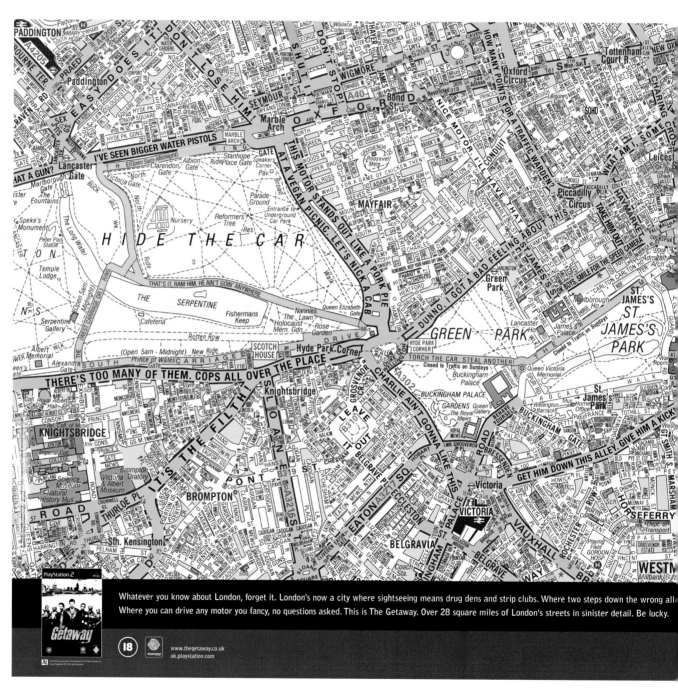

Whatever you know about London, forget it. London's now a city where sightseeing means drug dens and strip clubs. Where two steps down the wrong all
Where you can drive any motor you fancy, no questions asked. This is The Getaway. Over 28 square miles of London's streets in sinister detail. Be lucky.

www.thegetaway.co.uk
uk.playstation.com

90

These transformed vending machines were installed on university campuses and in shopping malls, making an ironic statement on the availability of guns in South Africa. Money placed in the slot went to a gun-free South Africa.

Client **KFM**
Agency **The Jupiter Drawing Room**
South Africa 2001

Installation the act of installing something

As a response to the 1987 American stock-market crash, the artist Arturo Di Modica wanted to pay tribute to the unceasing vitality of American capitalism. He did so by creating a sculpture. More specifically, he created a 7,000-pound bronze sculpture, which he funded with $360,000 of his own money. He even sold his family farm in Sicily to help pay for the project. During the night of 15 December 1989, Di Modica placed *Charging Bull* outside the New York Stock Exchange. In the morning, people were surprised to find a gigantic nostril-flaring bronze bull in the heart of New York's financial district, a reaction much like the amazement of the Trojans on discovering a giant wooden horse on their shores. The bull was immediately removed from the site because it lacked proper city permits and the police put the illegal sculpture in a compound. Public support for the sculpture was so great, however, that on 20 December the New York City Department of Parks & Recreation arranged for the bull to have a stomping ground in Bowling Green, the city's oldest park. There, it quickly became one of the most photographed and widely enjoyed pieces of public art in New York. And, when the local media reported on an upturn in the financial market, the bull became a standard picture accompanying the story.

The story of Di Modica's bronze bull demonstrates the power of installations. While the technique of transformation always starts from existing everyday objects or places and adds a twist to them, installations come out of nowhere and can take absolutely anything as a source of inspiration. A bronze bull is not a familiar sight on the streets of New York's financial district. **An installation has no boundaries or rules and can be made from any material, take any shape or size and be placed in any location, without having to refer to anything real.**

Installations are well suited to advertising purposes for several reasons. First, installations occupy space, their three-dimensional nature ensuring they are hard to ignore. For example, in 2005, Christo and Jeanne-Claude installed thousands of saffron-coloured gates in New York's Central Park. The installation, called *The Gates*, did not subtly alter the look of the park, it dramatically changed it. Second, as a result of their three-dimensional nature and their integration into the street scene, installations generally allow the visitor to interact with the work. They beg to be stared at, touched, climbed on, played with. This is not an essential reason for their construction, but a welcome bonus. The majority of the pictures of the *Charging Bull* in New York feature people sitting on the bull, holding its horns or just touching it. Furthermore, *The Gates* in Central Park were deliberately installed along 23 miles of pedestrian paths, allowing visitors to actually walk through the installation. **While traditional outdoor advertising campaigns remain passive and remote, installations allow brand messages to take on a three-dimensional life and to be fully integrated into the street scene.**

On Cape Town's busiest beach, this installation focused awareness on the city's water shortage and demonstrated the amount of water wasted in a single shower.

Client **City of Cape Town**
Agency **Ogilvy & Mather, Rightford Searle-Tripp & Makin**
South Africa 2003

92–95

Absolut Vodka's iconic bottle shape has become legendary through its print advertising campaigns. Here it proves that its main asset is equally able to lead a three-dimensional life.

This giant retro-style record player featured a pickup in the shape of the Absolut bottle. Fully illuminated, 6 x 6 metres in size, with revolving turntable and moving tone arm, it hung above a bar in the borough of Friedrichshain – home to Berlin's famous music and DJ scene – for a month.

Client **Absolut Vodka**
Agency **TBWA\Germany**
Germany 2004

An Absolut Chilled Igloo emphasized the fact that 'when drinking Absolut Vodka at home, remember it's best served at 0°C'. So, the perfect home in which to drink the vodka must be an igloo, where it is constantly 0°C. The igloo interior featured ice sculptures that re-created the appearance of an average British living room stocked with a cabinet of Absolut.

Client **Absolut Vodka**
Agency **TBWA\London**
UK 2003

Showing an understanding of the New York lifestyle, Absolut Vodka fitted a typical New York apartment within the shape of its bottle.

Client **Absolut Vodka**
Agency **TBWA\Chiat Day**
USA 2001

An Absolut oven stood with a
blazing fire and real heating
for over a month in the heart
of Prenzlauer Berg, Berlin's
artistic quarter, and the only
area that still heats with
traditional coal ovens.

Client **Absolut Vodka**
Agency **TBWA\Germany**
Germany 2004

96

Eighteen living-room
installations appeared
overnight in parking spaces
in 12 cities across the
Netherlands to prove that
IKEA can make the most of
any space at minimal expense.
Each set up had a resident
eating breakfast, reading
the newspaper and chatting
to passers-by. Vouchers were
handed out to a limited
number of people, giving
them the right to 'steal' the
furniture and take it home.

Client **IKEA**
Agency **Strawberry Frog**
the Netherlands 2002

'When IKEA came to
Holland, it quickly
became known as the
quirky Swedish brand
with the colourful
furniture. We wanted
to go back to that.'

José Derks, communication
manager, IKEA

97

Inciting people to tidy up their homes and get ready for the arrival of a new IKEA store, IKEA positioned yellow skips all over the city of Oslo.

Client **IKEA**
Agency **New Deal DDB**
Norway 2002

98

To promote its crazy prices on mattresses, IKEA used the product itself as a communication tool. Eighty-one mattresses were suspended in the train stations of major French cities, while another 38 graced the city centres.

Client **IKEA**
Agency **Ubi Bene**
France 2004

99

Designer Frank Tjepkema
helped to create garden-
themed Hoegaarden sampling
installations that positioned
the white beer as a unique and
natural drink to refresh the
mind. The collection comprised
quirky pieces, such as a nut
dispenser in the shape of a bird
feeder and a DJ booth covered
in grass. The installations
appeared at fashion events
throughout the summer in
Canada, the Czech Republic
and the UK.

Client **Interbrew**
Agency **Strawberry Frog**
2002

100

Tombstones carrying 'unusual'
epitaphs about street children
were placed on railway
platforms and pavements and
in parks – the places these
children call home. During
the campaign, donations
to Childline increased and
inquiries rose from around 600
to over 1600 calls per week.

Client **Childline India
Foundation**
Agency **Saatchi & Saatchi**
India 2004

101 & 102

Consistent with Mini Cooper's
playful image, these
installations in the USA and
Singapore emphasized the
Mini as the ultimate toy car.

Client **Mini Cooper**
Agency **Crispin Porter +
Bogusky**
USA 2003

Client **Mini Cooper**
Agency **TBWA\Singapore**
Singapore 2004

103

Taking literally the idea that if people were no longer going to church, the church would go to the people, the Protestant Church in Germany went on tour with a specially designed rubber church. The installation was erected in various public places to meet as many lost sheep as possible. The bishop personally conducted services at each location. In total, the inflatable church attracted 60,000 visitors.

Client **The Protestant Church**
Agency **Jung von Matt**
Germany 2004

104

Large numbers of mosquitoes are found on the Brazilian coast during the summer months. In an effort to go where the enemy was, a team of Brazilian and foreign sculptors created gigantic sand sculptures of mosquitoes on various beaches. Next to the sculptures, a banner offered the advice: 'Mosquitoes are all over the place. Better use SBP.'

Client **Clorox**
Agency **DM9DDB**
Brazil 2003

105

Gevalia coffee is famous for its enduring advertising campaign based on the theme of unexpected visitors, yet the branding seemed to be lacking 'urban visibility'. To remedy this, these outdoor installations appeared overnight, continuing the theme on the city streets in a rather extravagant way, although the branding was very subtle in keeping with the idea of an unexpected visit. The campaigns appeared in Gothenburg, Malmö and Stockholm.

Client **Kraft Foods**
Agency **Hall & Cederquist/Y&R**
Sweden 1995–96

AMPLIFICATION EFFECT
The installation was at the centre of the campaign, but other actions, such as radio commercials and in-store posters, helped to create the overall effect.

106

A 15-ton replica of a cookie landed UFO-style in London's Trafalgar Square to mark the launch of the 'Unbelievably Fudgy Object' biscuit by Maryland Cookies.

Client **Maryland Cookies**
Agency **Cunning**
UK 1999

107

In the busiest shopping areas of three German cities, 1-ton ice blocks with Wrangler jeans visibly frozen inside rested on the damaged roofs of cars, as if they had fallen from the sky. Pedestrians gathered around the ice, played with it, touched it, chopped it and even tried to remove the frozen jeans.

The installations were the central component of an integrated 'Ice Invasion' campaign – comprising multi-storey billboards, street posters and in-store communication – to promote the Fall/Winter 2004 collection.

Client **Wrangler**
Agency **BSUR**
Germany 2004

AMPLIFICATION EFFECT
Promotional teams took Polaroid pictures of the onlookers and encouraged them to go to Wrangler retailers where, upon presentation of the photo, they received a free T-shirt that said, 'I was a part of the Wrangler Ice Invasion'. Their pictures were also placed in the window displays.

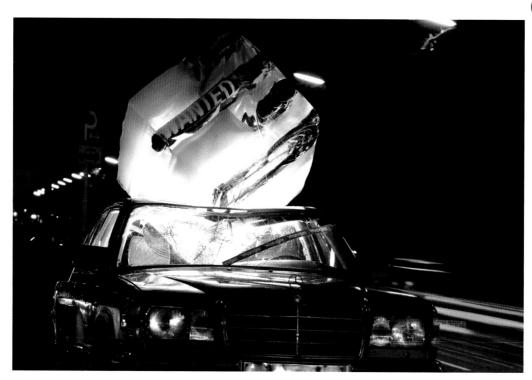

109

For its German launch, the Smart Forfour car went underground, literally. Passengers waiting on the underground platform were caught by surprise when they saw the new Smart Forfour model pulling into the station on freight-train wagons. The banner announced: 'Now also on the streets. The new Smart Forfour.'

Client **DaimlerChrysler**
Agency **Springer & Jacoby**
Germany 2004

108

To illustrate their leading position in the home-loans market, Washington Mutual Home Loans erected a series of attention-grabbing house structures in the heart of Chicago. The installations were refreshed every few months.

Client **Washington Mutual Home Loans**
Agency **Universal McCann**
USA 2003

Illusion communication that distorts our perception of what is real and what is not

When David Copperfield, one of the world's most popular illusionists, makes a train disappear in front of an audience simply by gesturing and pulling a cord, we know that we have been fooled. What we do not know is how. Although we may feel stupid or tricked, we go home puzzling over how on earth he pulled it off. Illusions fascinate us because they invite us to discover how we have been tricked. That is why we love magic shows. That is why we love illusions.

Illusions distort our perception of what is real and what is not. They make something unreal look, feel or seem like it is real. To do this, rather than distorting reality, illusions imitate reality. **The purpose of an illusion is to make us believe, if only for a fraction of a second, that what we are looking at exists or is actually happening.**

Advertising people have a lot in common with the illusionists and magicians of this world. Both try to make us believe that what is happening on the stage or screen is real; both divert our attention in one direction, while doing a trick in another; both take advantage of the limits of human perception. In short, both are in the business of deception and make-believe.

What makes the technique attractive for advertising purposes is that, as viewers, we need time to discover the illusion. Illusionist advertising confuses us about its true nature, provoking such reactions as: 'Is this actually happening? Am I seeing this correctly? Is this true?'. For a while at least, it has us fooled. **It is advertising of the second glance, requiring two steps, two glances to fully understand what it is.** Most advertising only receives one glance, which is sufficient to check out the true nature of the advert before we proceed on our way. A good illusion demands two glances: the first to notice it, the second to fully grasp it. In a world where attention is hard to come by, a second glance is worth its weight in gold.

The time between the two glances depends on how inventive and how realistic the illusion is and on the sort of illusion. With visuals or images, the second glance can come after a matter of seconds. Stories are a lot more sophisticated and more difficult to decode, so a much longer time can elapse before we discover whether they are true or not.

There are four ways in which we can create confusion between what is real and what is not:

- **False copies**
- **False perspectives**
- **False stories**
- **False perceptions**

False copies

Anyone who has visited Madame Tussauds in London is familiar with the thrill of watching a world-famous icon appear before their eyes. The museum's detailed wax replicas make visitors think the personalities are standing there for real. To achieve this, the makers of the wax statues simulate as closely as possible every single detail of the original person.

This illustrates the most drastic way to create confusion between what is real and what is not: by copying reality. By creating perfect simulations of reality, it becomes difficult to judge whether something is real or not. The rule is simple: the better the copy, the greater the confusion.

110

Since its debut on MTV, *jackass* has become synonymous with self-inflicted pain and gross gags. One week before the show started its infamous run on MTV, life-size dummies brought the heart and soul of the programme to the streets, creating the illusion that real people were stuck in drains and bins.

Client **MTV**
Agency **Age Comunicação**
Brazil 2004

111

Harsh screams from a tortured man blared out from under the grates on a busy shopping street. Instinctively, pedestrians looked down and read: 'Today 133 journalists are imprisoned and tortured all over the world'.

Client **Reporters Without Borders**
Agency **DDB**
Belgium 2003

112

A life-size mannequin of a child was placed on top of a bus shelter. It carried a sound device that emitted crying, creating the illusion that a child was trapped there. The accompanying billboard said: 'He is your son. Be helpful to others just like they are your loved ones.' This misleading trick was part of a campaign to promote ING's caring attitude, which is the financial institution's main communication platform in Hong Kong.

Client **ING**
Agency **BBDO Hong Kong**
China 2002

AMPLIFICATION EFFECT
The action was front-page news in the first and third most popular newspapers in Hong Kong. It was also covered in the newspaper with the second largest readership. This equalled a total media value of around US $130,000, ten times the budget of the campaign.

113

To promote the 'Out-in-Africa Gay & Lesbian Film Festival', the familiar expression 'coming out of the closet' was taken literally. A chained closet, with the sign 'Opening Soon', was put up in the foyer of the cinema complex for two weeks prior to the festival. What attracted most attention was the recording of random knocking and screaming that was played from inside the closet, creating the illusion that actual people were trapped within and eager to come out.

Client **Nedbank**
Agency **The Jupiter Drawing Room**
South Africa 2001

Fake coffee stains soiled the pages of a newspaper in a campaign for the launch of the new Real Café packaging. People were left with the impression that someone else had already read their paper before them.

On the first page, round coffee stains, as if from the bottom of a cup, appeared on top of the news with the statement: 'There was a little gift for you here, but it looks like someone else got to it first'.

The next page had coffee drops on top of the news with the phrase: 'Not again! Turn the page quickly, there's still one more.'

On the final page, a sachet was glued to the page with the message: 'Ah! At last! This new look has made us irresistible. Now also in a refill and a sachet.'

Client **Real Café**
Agency **Prisma Propaganda**
Brazil 2003

115

Wigs were placed on sewer
and metro grates in Paris to
create the effect that these
women were so thin, thanks
to eating Amora Light
mayonnaise, that they had
fallen through the holes.

Client **Amora**
Agency **TBWA\Paris**
France 2004

116

False crime scenes took advantage of people's morbid curiosity, drawing them close enough to communicate details about the upcoming season of the forensic drama *CSI: Crime Scene Investigation.*

Client **AXN**
Agency **Saatchi & Saatchi**
Singapore 2004

117

Zuji is Singapore's one-stop travel portal. To drive people to the website, mock travel guides, travel magazines and city maps were placed alongside real ones at leading bookstores. On the outside, the design and copy looked authentic; inside, nothing but the Zuji website and tagline were printed on every page.

Client **Zuji**
Agency **M&C Saatchi**
Singapore 2004

118

Nike's new football concept was called Scorpion Knock Out (SKO) as it revolved around the idea of 'quick touch, precise touch, deadly touch'. To promote these new football rules, 50 fake bear traps were left in playgrounds, parks and schools where football was played at weekends, with a football as decoy.

Two weeks later, the teaser was revealed and posters with the Scorpion Knock Out logo were put up in the same places as the traps had been laid. Visits to the website rocketed after the campaign.

Client **Nike**
Agency **BBDO Argentina**
Argentina 2002

119

For a 'don't drink and drive' campaign, a magnetic keyhole was placed beside the real one on the driver's door of vehicles parked outside drinking establishments. When drivers returned to their cars, they thought they were seeing double. A message on the reverse of the keyhole urged drivers to consider whether they were in a fit state to drive.

Client **Guinness UDV**
Agency **Saatchi & Saatchi**
South Africa 2003

AMPLIFICATION EFFECT
The media coverage on this campaign was valued at US $25,000.

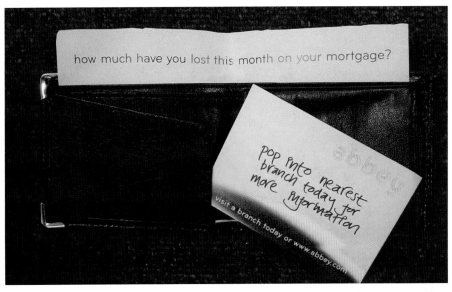

120

Human rights are still being trampled underfoot. To illustrate this, mock hands were attached to sewer grates in the middle of a busy shopping district in Germany, clinging to the bars as if in a prison cell. The words 'wrong faith', 'wrong colour' or 'wrong opinion' were tattooed on the fingers to remind passers-by of the unjust reasons people are kept behind bars.

Client **Amnesty International**
Agency **Leo Burnett GmbH**
Germany 2003

121

Several thousand ordinary leather wallets were dropped across a number of UK cities in places where it would seem like an accident, such as the inside of taxis, in changing rooms in clothes shops and on the top deck of double-decker buses. Poking out of the top of each wallet was what appeared to be a £50 note. Who could resist picking it up to examine it – whether for honest reasons or not? Inside the wallet a message read: 'How much have you lost this month on your mortgage?'. The aim was to confront people's financial apathy. Most people happily ignore the rate they pay on their mortgage and yet would feel devastated if they lost £50, even though the amount wasted every month on the wrong mortgage can be far more.

Client **Abbey**
Agency **Naked Communications**
UK 2003

Snow?

The C-Class.
Now with permanent 4-wheel drive.

Mercedes-Benz
Die Zukunft des Automobils.

www.mercedes-benz.de

122

During a commercial break in Germany, television viewers suddenly experienced picture interference, also known as 'screen snow'. When they began to suspect that their television set was having reception problems, two headlights suddenly appeared in the midst of the interference. They gradually drew nearer until a car finally emerged from the snowstorm. Only when the car came right up to the camera were viewers able to see it was the Mercedes-Benz C-Class four-wheel drive.

Client **Mercedes-Benz**
Agency **Springer & Jacoby Werbung**
Germany 2003

123

This is a great example of faith in your own product! 3M demonstrated the strength of their new security glass by encasing 83-million Canadian dollars, mostly fake but with real bills on the top, in a bus shelter poster space made from their glass. Passers-by, desperate for the money, put the glass to the test by kicking it and taking sledgehammers to it. The glass withstood the pressure and did not shatter. Only the aluminium frame was breached, at which point security guards called a halt to proceedings as it was regarded as cheating.

Client **Trim Line**
Agency **Rethink Communications**
Canada 2005

AMPLIFICATION EFFECT

Canadian local and national news shows reported on the crazy attempts to get the cash. Considering that there were only 500 real dollars in the case and the poster site had only been rented for a day, the campaign proved to be great value for money.

124

Special stickers, giving the impression of condensation caused by a steaming cup of soup were placed on train windows. In the condensation was written 'Knorr Cup Soup', as if it had been finger-written by passengers. These winter ads were placed on trains that went through cold, snowy regions. For a budget of only US $10,000, approximately 600,000 passengers were exposed to the advertising.

Client **Ajinomoto Co./Knorr**
Agency **Hakuhodo**
Japan 2005

False perspectives

In the *Naturalis Historia*, Pliny, the Roman author and philosopher, related the story of a contest between two Greek painters, Zeuxis and Parrhasius, in the fifth century BC to determine who was the better artist. Zeuxis painted grapes so realistically that birds flew down to peck them. Parrhasius then asked Zeuxis to draw back the curtain to display his picture. When Zeuxis discovered that the curtain itself was Parrhasius's work, he admitted defeat for although his work had deceived the birds, Parrhasius's had tricked the eyes of an artist.

This contest reveals a subtle method for creating optical illusions: two-dimensional images that suggest depth and trick our sense of perspective. This tactic proved particularly popular in the production of trompe l'oeils. French for 'deception of the eye', trompe-l'oeil paintings are conceived in a deliberate attempt to create the illusion of three dimensions. The main technical trick is to apply the right shadows to suggest depth without the eye seeing actual depth.

The suggestion of depth was also one of the key features in early cinema. In 1895, when the brothers Lumière projected *The Arrival of a Train* on a large screen in a Paris salon, the audience was reportedly so frightened by the image of a train coming directly at them that they screamed and ran to the back of the room. The technique has also been exploited repeatedly for comic purposes, specifically in cartoons. In a classic Roadrunner cartoon scene, the Coyote paints a picture of a tunnel on the side of a mountain and sniggers as the Roadrunner approaches at top speed. Instead of smashing into the rock, the Roadrunner gives his 'meep meep' and runs through the tunnel. Puzzled, the Coyote studies his painting and a truck roars out of the tunnel and flattens him.

Outdoor advertising, often condemned to the sad world of two dimensions, is only too glad to embrace optical illusions, knowing they can enhance the level of realism and incite people, in a moment of confusion, to give the message a second glance.

125

A drawing on a highly frequented square made it look as if the new Smart Forfour had already hit the streets.

Client **DaimlerChrysler**
Agency **Springer & Jacoby**
Germany 2004

126

Using the motto 'surprisingly spacious', these sun shields made people do a double take at the interiors advertising the Smart car.

Client **DaimlerChrysler**
Agency **Springer & Jacoby**
Germany 2004

127

In-store advertisements
suggested that pets would take
the most drastic measures
to obtain their favourite
food brand.

Client **Purina**
Agency **McCann-Erickson**
Brazil 2004

AMPLIFICATION EFFECT
The T-shirts were distributed at parties to trendsetters and given away to regular partygoers as long as they were willing to have their photograph taken in the T-shirt. The pictures were turned into Hakle adverts in lifestyle and party magazines to build awareness among the young.

128

These clean buttocks printed on the back of a T-shirt created the illusion that the person wearing the T-shirt had his or her bottom exposed. It was the ideal gimmick for a fun-loving party crowd and perfectly in keeping with toilet-paper brand Hakle's core proposition, 'for absolute cleanliness'.

Client **Hakle-Kimberly Switzerland GmbH**
Agency **Advico Young & Rubicam Zurich**
Switzerland 2004

129

The styles of new Foschini handbags were printed on transparent shopping bags to make it seem as if every woman coming out of the store had bought herself a bag.

Client **Foschini**
Agency **The Jupiter Drawing Room**
South Africa 2002

130

A sticker on the outside of a double-decker bus was enough to change it into the magical purple triple-decker Knight Bus from the Harry Potter movie *The Prisoner of Azkaban*. During Singapore's two-week school holiday, the bus offered youngsters activity-filled 30-minute rides to promote the opening of the film.

Client **Warner Bros.**
Agency **Mediaedge:CIA**
Singapore 2004

131

For a period of time in a park
popular with long-distance
runners, construction work
resulted in the path ending
abruptly at a hoarding.
Nike, a brand that is all
about surpassing boundaries,
grabbed the opportunity to
place a poster on the fencing
to create the illusion that the
road continued.

Client **Nike**
Agency **Ogilvy & Mather**
Singapore 2004

132
Transparent guerrilla ads on windows, walls and pavements promoted the 'X-Files' television series on the South African channel SABC 2 by suggesting an alien presence.

Client **SABC 2**
Agency **TBWA\Hunt Lascaris**
South Africa 2004

133

On approaching your car, you would think that yet another flyer had been put under your wiper. However, these flyers on cars parked near schools had a rather shocking image printed on the reverse, confronting drivers with the potential consequences of speeding.

Client **Environment Waikato**
Agency **Colenso BBDO**
New Zealand 2004

PLEASE DON'T SPEED NEAR SCHOOLS

134

This special billboard made it look as if the Audi Allroad was truly living up to its name.

Client **Senna Import**
Agency **Almap BBDO**
Brazil 2001

135

This sandwich board made the man carrying it look like a landmine victim, a visual trick to draw people's attention (as well as their money) to the cause.

Client **German Initiative to Ban Landmines**
Agency **Scholz & Friends**
Germany 2004

136

Football star Thierry Henry seemed to be using this famous Parisian square as his training ground. An 80m-long image of the star in action graced the wall of a building on one side of the square. On the opposite side, a gigantic, three-dimensional ball seemed to be crashing through the front of a building.

Client **Nike**
Agency **Ubi Bene**
France 2004

137

By using full-size images of the Brandenburg Gate during the gate's 24-month restoration period, Deutsche Telekom billboards tricked the people of Berlin into thinking that their monument had not completely disappeared from sight. It was also this campaign that finally persuaded the Berlin Senate – who owned the gate – to give their go-ahead to use it for advertising purposes.

Client **T-Mobile**
Agency **Springer & Jacoby Media**
Germany 2003

138

Photographs in and around railway stations gave the impression that real facilities – toilets, plug sockets, elevators and monitors – were available to travellers. The illusions confronted people with the consequences of fraud on public transport.

Client **SNCF**
Agency **TBWA\Paris**
France 2002

139

IKEA wanted to convince its target group that its catchphrase, 'change is easy', was not a hollow promise. With a view to showing how easy it was to improve a living environment by going to IKEA, the company selected 20 multi-storey residential buildings. Inside, branded elevators gave people the illusion of going down or up in a completely changed space. IKEA furniture was also installed for the elevator assistants, who distributed catalogues and directed residents to the stores.

Client **IKEA**
Agency **Mediaedge:CIA**
China 2004

 AMPLIFICATION EFFECT
The elevator campaign spread quickly by word of mouth and generated a lot of free publicity.

140

Cleverly placed advertisements
for the International
Foundation of Human Rights
gave people the feeling of
unwillingly torturing others
while carrying out their
routine actions.

Client **International
Foundation of
Human Rights**
Agency **Jung von Matt**
Germany 2003

141

Trompe l'oeils turned the stripes on ordinary pedestrian crossings into the appearance of bodies wrapped in white sheets. They were positioned at major intersections throughout several European cities on the day of the annual European Road Safety Conference. Reminding pedestrians of their behaviour behind the wheel, they read: 'Every year, 7000 pedestrians are killed throughout Europe. Think about it when you're driving.'

Client **Responsible Young Drivers**
Agency **TBWA\Paris**
France 2004

False stories

Prior to the adoption of the Gregorian calendar, the new year began on 1 April and was celebrated in much the same way as it is today with parties and dancing into the late hours. In 1582, Pope Gregory XIII introduced the Gregorian calendar for the Christian world and the new year fell on 1 January. Some people, however, had not heard or did not believe the change of date and continued to celebrate on 1 April. Others played tricks on them and called them 'April fools', sending them on a fool's errand or trying to make them believe an untruth.

In most countries today, people still play small tricks on friends and strangers on 1 April. Aside from simple tricks, such as telling someone their shoelace is undone, there have been much more spectacular deceptions. On 1 April 1957, one of the most famous tricks occurred when the UK BBC television programme *Panorama* broadcast a documentary on the Swiss harvesting spaghetti from trees. **The success of this story, and all false stories that are perceived as real, depends on four factors: a plausible story, a convincing style, a credible source and tangible proof.**

First, the story needs to be plausible, but not necessarily realistic. *Panorama* did not announce that spaghetti suddenly grew on trees without any further explanation or augmentation. It put down the phenomenon to a very mild winter and 'the virtual disappearance of the spaghetti weevil, the tiny creature whose depredations have caused much concern in the past'. The story also anticipated viewers' questions; for instance, why, if spaghetti grows on trees, does it always come in uniform lengths? The answer was that it was 'the result of many years of patient endeavour by past breeders who succeeded in producing the perfect spaghetti'.

Second, the style in which the story is told needs to be convincing. *Panorama* was in a documentary style and the audience heard Richard Dimbleby, the show's highly respected commentator, discuss details of the spaghetti crop. 'The spaghetti harvest here in Switzerland is not, of course, carried out on anything like the tremendous scale of the Italian industry,' Dimbleby informed the audience, 'Many of you, I'm sure, will have seen pictures of the vast spaghetti plantations in the Po valley. For the Swiss, however, it tends to be more of a family affair.'

Third, the source that spreads the story needs to be credible. In the case of the spaghetti trees, *Panorama* is considered a prestigious programme. The general trust that was still placed in the medium of television also lent the claim credibility.

Finally, the story needs tangible proof. In the *Panorama* episode, viewers saw footage of a rural Swiss family pulling down strands of spaghetti from trees and placing them in baskets.

Since the spaghetti tree story perfectly adhered to these four criteria, a huge number of viewers were duped. Many called up wanting to know how they could grow their own spaghetti trees, to which the BBC diplomatically replied that they should 'place a sprig of spaghetti in a tin of tomato sauce and hope for the best'. These four criteria do not need to appear in equal measure. The less plausible the content, the more credible the source needs to be and the more realistic the style in which it is told. On the other hand, the more tangible proof there is to back up the story, the less plausible it needs to be.

When it comes to conventional advertising, all four factors face something of a problem. First, advertising messages are rarely plausible. Advertising is a world of superlatives, excessive claims and overstatements. Second, the style in which the messages are conveyed can seem very false and, therefore, unconvincing. Third, advertising commercials are not by nature very credible. As Al and Laura Ries state in *The Fall of Advertising and the Rise of PR*, an advertising message 'is perceived to be one-sided, biased, selfish, and company-oriented rather than consumer-oriented'. Fourth, for many products, there is little tangible proof behind the excessive claims of eternal youth or exciting lives.

As a consequence, some brands have opted for the hidden power of false stories to bypass the heightened level of scepticism towards advertising. In the last few years, an increasing number of false stories have come to light that were spoofs orchestrated by brands or companies. Much like April fools' jokes, false stories are only worthwhile if they continue to be funny, interesting or, above all, relevant once their true nature has been discovered. Otherwise, they are nothing but a nuisance, or worse, plain boring. What follows are some inspiring examples of stories that fulfil these specifications and tread a fine line between fiction and reality, between what we perceive as true or false.

142

When playing the PlayStation2 version of *Formula One*, your games can be logged on the Web for others to see how well you play. This led to the idea of players having fans, just as drivers do in the real Formula One. For the launch of the game, a personalized letter in the handwriting of a young boy, who seemed to be an obsessive Italian fan, was created. Only as the recipient read on did it become apparent from the branding and the offers that it was in fact from Sony PlayStation.

People's awareness and intimate recall of the piece reached almost 50% and sales doubled at participating retailers immediately after the mailing went out, while sales at other retailers remained flat.

Client **PlayStation**
Agency **ClaydonHeeley JonesMason**
UK 2001

143

For the launch of Sega's National Football League game, an elaborate fiction was woven based on the game's special feature: a first-person view of the football action. Revolving around a focus group member of the Sega game, called Beta-7, the story claimed that playing the game led to blackouts and violent behaviour, which Sega was trying to cover up. This is how the story unfolded through a variety of media channels.

1 Beta-7 posted queries on game editorial sites asking whether other Beta testers for Sega's game were also experiencing blackouts and aggressive impulses.

2 Beta-7.com was launched as a blog chronicling the tester's odd side effects and his battle with Sega. The site offered plenty of tangible proof to back up the story, among which was his invitation to the Sega focus group and video clips of other gamers blacking out after playing. The site also contained a discussion board for others to join in.

3 Beta-X, a secret source within Sega, leaked shredded Sega documents and stolen copies of the game to Beta-7. The documents revealed that Sega had been aware of the problems with the game for months.

4 Copies of the game were sent to nine real gamers, asking them whether they could figure out what was going on.

5 Small ads appeared in newspapers across the country asking if anybody had joined the Sega focus groups.

6 To get non-believers to reconsider, or at least to keep them hooked, the marketers took down the Beta-7 website, supposedly in response to a cease and desist order from Sega itself.

7 A rival Beta tester's blog was devised – gamerchuck.com – which denounced Beta-7 as a liar. With loads of game footage, gamerchuck was made to seem like a thinly veiled Sega PR stunt.

8 Homemade video clips were put on the Beta-7 site – again online – showing how people from Sega were being ambushed and confronted.

9 Beta-13, another focus group member who experienced the same nasty side effects after playing the game, came by some incriminating documents taken out of the bins at Sega.

10 On segasports.com, a letter was published in which Sega denied all accusations.

11 A disclaimer was added to the Sega television commercial saying: 'Excessive video game playing will not lead to violent or erratic behavior'.

12 A video clip was posted on espnsports.com in which Warren Sapp, who featured in the Sega television commercial, advised gamers not to try any of the game's moves at home.

13 Beta-X, supposedly a secret source from within Sega, came up with some decisive proof against Sega. He posted a link to a classified internal medical website, revealing information and pictures of people's physical injuries as a result of playing the game.

14 Fake blogs from individual fans were created, linking all the pieces of the puzzle and thereby fuelling the debate.

15 Two days before the launch of the game, Beta-13 urged Beta-7 to come to San Francisco, where he lived, since he had the definitive evidence against Sega. Yet Beta-7 never arrived. His apartment was ransacked by people from Sega. This is where the story ended.

Despite the elaborate proof and the very convincing way in which the story unfolded, a great many visitors to Beta-7 and its spin-off sites recognized the campaign as a marketing ploy. In one poll taken during the campaign, about 60% recognized it for what it was. Nevertheless, users were attracted to the seamless nature of the fiction and thought it clever enough to follow. Unlike most marketing campaigns, the entirety of the campaign was not fully imagined at its inception, because the creators added new elements in response to visitor reaction.

Client **Sega**
Agency **Wieden + Kennedy**
USA 2004

'The process for creating Beta-7 was much more like theatre or film production than Web development.'

Ty Montague, Wieden + Kennedy

144

Le Soir, the most respected newspaper in French-speaking Belgium, took the launch of its new format as an opportunity to stress its progressive attitude and to comment on some questionable evolutions in contemporary society. In a most controversial and teasing campaign, the paper launched three fake enterprises, each one dealing with very sensitive subject matters linked to current events: babyforeveryone.com, which sold babies online; Give Life, which sold organs from the third world; and the Institute of Integration, which sold services to integrate immigrants,

including products to whiten skin and to change eye colour. The three companies were announced in a very realistic way through posters, television, radio and three different websites, without any signature from Le Soir.

After two days of national commotion, it was revealed that Le Soir was behind the initiative. The three issues at the centre of the campaign were then treated in-depth in the newspaper.

Client **Le Soir**
Agency **mortierbrigade**
Belgium 2005

AMPLIFICATION EFFECT
From the moment the three companies were launched, every news channel and newspaper in Belgium reported on these mysterious and alarming businesses. Several organizations and official authorities investigated the case, including the FBI, which ordered the websites to be taken offline.

145

In spring 2004, several odd sites popped up describing the efforts of a British scientist and retired engineer at BMW, Dr Colin Mayhew, to transform BMW Mini parts into various types of robots. Tangible proof included a book called *Men of Metal: Eyewitness Accounts of Humanoid Robots*, which reported the experiments and consisted of dated entries, short descriptions and recorded conversations. No concrete opinions or assumptions were offered, allowing the reader to draw their own conclusions as the mystery unfolded.

Information was scattered over five different websites and left people assuming that internal combustion robots were being built and tested in a remote area of England. Details, such as the statement that Mayhew's home consumed 10 times more electricity than most homes of its size, drew the reader into the story. Remarks about the story from robotics hobbyists and BMW and Mini Cooper enthusiasts were found on various message boards on the Internet.

This hoax was set up to create a stir around the new Mini site that allowed surfers to transform a Mini into a robot and to compose a Mini to their personal specification. Big Mini robots were also mounted in large cities.

The New York Times covered the story and was the first traditional media channel to break the story to the masses. The newspaper labelled the ad campaign as 'interactive fiction'.

Client **Mini**
Agency **Crispin Porter + Bogusky**
USA 2004

AMPLIFICATION EFFECT
The book was distributed during the New York Auto Show and at selected news-stands, where it was inserted into such magazines as *Rolling Stone*, *Men's Health*, *Men's Journal* and *Motor Trend*.

146

To measure existing prejudice towards Aids in Brazil, a social experiment was conducted. A sticker was attached to a seat in a crowded underground station, carrying the false message: 'Someone with Aids sat here'. A total of 174 people read the message and the majority of them elected not to sit on the chair. Six people even ripped the sticker. Only one person sat on the chair.

Client **Brazilian Ministry of Health**
Agency **Master JWT**
Brazil 2003

AMPLIFICATION EFFECT
People's genuine reactions to the false warning were filmed for a 12-hour period, clearly demonstrating that prejudices towards people with Aids were a fact. The film was shown in cinemas and was aired on the country's highest rating TV show to get the maximum out of the small investment.

147

Some false stories are around for quite some time before their phoney nature is revealed. This one, however, lasted only one hour. But it was a buzz-filled hour.

Most women have fantasized at some point about taking revenge on an ex-boyfriend, the best part of which is public humiliation. This insight was the basis for an illusion carried out by *nzgirl*, an online magazine for young girls. At The Big Day Out, New Zealand's largest outdoor music festival, a plane flew over a crowd of 45,000 people towing a banner with the message,

'Scott Kelly has got a small dick'. The response was instantaneous: girls were talking and texting as fast as their fingers allowed them. Guys were thinking, 'Thank God it's not me'. An hour later, a second plane towed a banner 'Don't mess with *nzgirls*. www.nzgirl.co.nz', revealing the true author behind the message.

Client *nzgirl*
Agency **DDB New Zealand**
New Zealand 2004

AMPLIFICATION EFFECT
A PR release was sent to all major media on the afternoon of The Big Day Out, alerting them to look skyward. National newspapers and radio stations covered the action. At precisely the same time as the first plane flew over people walked through the crowd wearing 'I'm Scott Kelly' T-shirts. Stickers bearing the same message were stuck on the backs of unsuspecting males in the crowd. A video camera recorded the action and sent it out virally that night to the 9,000-strong *nzgirl* database. It was voted the second best viral email worldwide by the British newspaper *The Sun*.

False perceptions

According to cognitive psychology, we create a model of how the world works when we move about in it. Yet, our perceptions are always provisional, constantly shifting when we acquire new information. This explains the effect of optical illusions, whereby one object can give rise to multiple, entirely separate and distinct perceptions. As the saying goes, things are not always as they appear.

While most advertising is characterized by its unequivocality, the following campaigns show examples of ambiguous visual imagery. One by one, they create false perceptions, making people reconsider what they have seen. These false perceptions create a prolonged attention span and heighten the element of surprise.

148

Yes, it is just a dog. But, a stiffened leash and a promotional message can make the imagination run wild. This action was implemented to promote the film *The Invisible Man*, which was showing on the New Zealand television channel TV3.

Client **TV3**
Agency **Colenso BBDO**
New Zealand 2001

149

Helium-filled 'missile' balloons were attached with nylon strings to a vehicle. When the truck was in motion, the balloons trailed it like heat-seeking missiles in endless pursuit of their target. This eye-catching trick was developed to promote the action programmes on Channel 9 and was part of the launch campaign for this new Malaysian television station.

Client **Channel 9**
Agency **J Walter Thompson Malaysia**
Malaysia 2004

150

Plant pots bearing the Paton Fertilizers name, were placed at the base of trees to give the illusion that the brand was living up to its catch line 'We make it grow'.

Client **Paton Fertilizers**
Agency **Publicis Mojo**
Australia 2004

151

To communicate its unique
view on business and world
events, *The Economist* rolled
out this giant 20-metre-long
mat in the business district.
When approached from the
right angle, it gave the illusion
of being square. The campaign
wanted to convey that
sometimes it takes a unique
approach to get things
in perspective.

Client **The Economist**
Agency **Ogilvy & Mather**
Singapore 2004

152

For the two million people who each month visit the Marunouchi Building, known as the Empire State Building of Tokyo, the beautiful view from The Observatory floor was disturbed when it became the basis for an environmental campaign. To raise awareness and to reinforce the message that the hole in the ozone layer must be prevented from growing, nine windows were covered with black stains representing the expanding hole. The stains were accurate renderings of NASA satellite imagery and conveyed the disturbing evolution of the ozone layer.

Client **The Mainichi Newspaper**
Agency **Hakuhodo**
Japan 2004

air zoom swift vapor
nikespeed.com

153

Wrapped around the building,
this advertisement for the Nike
Air Zoom Swift Vapor added
an illusory twist to the façade,
creating an impression of
extreme speed.

Client **Nike**
Agency **Ogilvy & Mather**
Taiwan 2004

154

To illustrate how much energy Lipton's Cup-A-Soup Asian Style offers its drinkers, a sated rickshaw driver seemingly pulled a huge lorry bearing the brand's message through downtown Toronto. Samples were given out en route to ensure everyone experienced the soup.

Client **Unilever Canada**
Agency **Zig**
Canada 2002

155

Very few people were enthusiastic about walking underneath this billboard at Hamburg Airport, which featured a Mercedes fixed upside down to the ceiling. The text read: 'Careful! Stuck together with cheap glue only. With great prices like ours, we can't afford better.'

Client **Sixt**
Agency **Jung von Matt**
Germany 2003

156

The clever combination of two separate elements – a billboard showing a Mini Cooper driving by at full speed and bent palm trees – forms the basis of this false perception. The palm trees seem to be bending back because the Mini is passing at such speed.

Client **Mini**
Agency **Crispin Porter + Bogusky**
USA 2003

157

Suspended from the post office, a huge postage stamp showed Legolas, the archer in *The Lord of the Rings*, taking aim. On the opposite side of the street, a gigantic three-dimensional arrow was embedded in the outside wall of a building. This street scene announced the launch of *The Lord of the Rings* stamps and proved to be a great success.

Client **New Zealand Post**
Agency **Saatchi & Saatchi**
New Zealand 2003

Keep an eye on the right hand side of the screen.

158

Suzuki gave new meaning
to the term 'widescreen' by
projecting part of their ad
outside the boundary of the
screen and onto the walls of
selected cinemas. The illusory
effect of a car leaving the
screen demonstrated the
4x4's off-road ability in a
manner unique to cinema.

Client **Delta Motor
Corporation**
Agency **Network BBDO**
South Africa 2004

159
The message 'If you can't read
this you're too close' was seen
clearly from a distance, but
the closer drivers got to the
back of the bus, the more the
type distorted until it became
indecipherable.

Client **Department
of Transport**
Agency **The Dukes of
Urbino.com**
South Africa 2004

Infiltration the use of people to penetrate an area

Before printed let alone electronic media became the standard way to transfer and spread news, the main carriers of information were people. From as early as Greek times, declarations of war or offers of surrender were taken between parties by heralds whose duty it was to deliver the message as quickly and as safely as possible. One of the most famous heralds was the Greek Phidippides. Legend has it that he ran the 26 miles from Marathon to Athens to announce the Greek victory in the Battle of Marathon in 5BC and died upon arrival. His tour de force was the origin of today's marathon. Somewhat less athletic carriers of news were the town criers or bellmen, who walked through a town ringing a hand bell and announcing news and proclamations. These 'historical newscasters' drew the attention of the mostly illiterate public to matters of importance. As town criers enjoyed royal protection, the command 'don't shoot the messenger' had very real significance. The crier would read a proclamation, usually at the door of the local inn, and then nail it to the door post, which is where the expression 'posting a notice' comes from.

The function these figures played in previous times has been taken over largely by official and organized media channels. **Although we have access to many different, almost instant, types of communication these days, human beings are still fantastic media, able to infiltrate new territories.** To start with, there are more than 6 billion potential 'media units' on this planet. And, since we are essentially social creatures, we are constantly in touch with each other. We like looking at other people; we like observing how others look, walk, speak, act. People, therefore, are a natural source of attention. Furthermore, people have the advantage of being highly mobile and highly flexible. While most media are fixed and static, people move freely in and adjust to any given environment. Most importantly, however, people communicate in many different ways. They can come in the form of promotion teams, sandwich-board men, actors, brand ambassadors, street teams, product endorsers, spokespersons, and so on. Two categories are easily distinguishable in the use of people for infiltration purposes: carriers and performers.

Using people as carriers

Carriers are people who literally 'carry' messages, almost like empty vessels that can be branded for any occasion. These are people who lend their voice or body for the noble purpose of advertising, spreading messages to anybody they encounter. Sandwich-board men and promotion teams are classic examples. Today, still, a sandwich board in a busy area is guaranteed to attract the attention of passers-by — even if they are not interested, they always read the message, much like the written signs beggars hold up. The person carrying the message makes us assume there is something personal to impart.

The latest trend is to use people's own bodies as advertising space. It started with foreheads, the most logical and eye-catching place on somebody's body, but it has since involved bottoms and even pregnant bellies.

A more subtle way of using people as carriers is when everyday consumers promote products unbeknownst to the people with

whom they come into contact. The process is simple: companies give consumers free products or goodies and, in exchange, consumers are seen publicly with them and talk about them to friends, acquaintances and strangers. The more people see a product being used in public or the more they hear about it from people they know and trust, the more likely they are to buy it for themselves.[11] To give an indication of where and how the information on a product spreads, these consumers often file reports on their interactions to the company that hires them. The basic premise is that there is nothing more powerful than a personal recommendation by a friend or acquaintance; the conversations we have in our everyday lives.[12] This form of marketing goes by a host of titles, including exponential, wildfire, domino, organic, word-of-mouth, word of mouse and referral marketing.[13] Whatever its title, it turns people's everyday conversations and actions into the newest medium.

160

In an attempt to convince people to fasten their seat belts, disabled people were hired in Santiago to put forward some persuasive arguments. They approached car drivers who were not wearing their seat belts with flyers saying: 'I didn't buckle my seat belt either'. Nine out of 10 drivers immediately fastened their belt. The confrontational nature of the action ensured that it became the talk of the town.

Client **Carabineros de Chile**
Agency **Grey Worldwide Chile**
Chile 2003

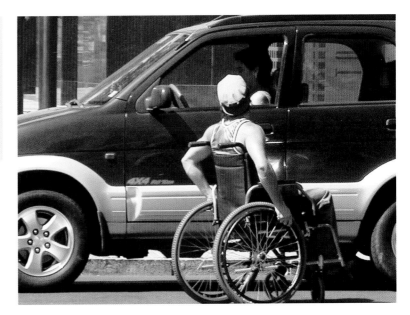

161

Devised by Fathom Communications, these actions to promote the Sony Ericsson T68i, a mobile phone and digital camera, stirred heavy debate within marketing and communication circles about the boundaries of undercover tactics.

In one initiative, dubbed 'Fake Tourist', trained actors and actresses pretended to be tourists, asking unsuspecting passers-by to take their pictures with their Sony Ericsson T68i. The idea was to make onlookers think they had stumbled across a hot new product. Some called the tactic deceptive, but Fathom Communications president Peter Groome insisted that it was not 'undercover' selling, because the actors simply demonstrated the product and did not give a sales pitch.

A second phase involved 60 actresses and female models who frequented trendy lounges and bars, where they played out scripted scenarios designed to help them engage strangers in conversation. One involved the actress's phone ringing and the caller's picture popping up on the screen. In another scenario, two women sit at opposite ends of the bar playing an interactive version of the Battleship game on their phones.

Client **Sony Ericsson Mobile Communications Ltd**
Agency **Fathom Communications**
USA 2002

162

To challenge people's perception of whiteness in a live and comparative way, an Ace promotional team put a small white sticker on people's white garments. This 2-second demonstration was accompanied with a sample of Ace washing powder.

Client **Procter & Gamble**
Agency **Leo Burnett Chile**
Chile 2004

163

Dunlop Tyres sent out
'treadheads' – people whose
hair was shaved in a tyre
pattern – to roam the streets
of Boston and exude coolness
in an attempt to reach the
younger generation.

Client **Dunlop**
Agency **Street Attack**
USA 2003

Using people as performers

Performers do not just carry a message, they dramatize it and turn it into an act. By adding an element of theatre, performers gain people's attention through their actions. Also referred to as 'street theatre' or 'performance advertising', performers return to the traditions of jugglers, magicians, storytellers, puppeteers, acrobats, clowns and mime artists, people trained to mesmerize crowds through their skills and abilities.

In *The Experience Economy*, Pine and Gilmore quote a doctoral student in performance studies on the way street artists assemble their audience: 'The street performer succeeds in transforming urban space into a theater place, turning visitors resting on steps into an audience seated on bleachers.'[14] Carriers can only hope to gather a maximum number of looks from passers-by, they do not have the originality and added value to assemble crowds. Carriers announce, performers entertain. Entertainment turns a random number of individuals into a group and an urban space into a theatre.

Of course, street performances reach a limited number of people, but they are an ideal catalyst for word-of-mouth advertising. People who were unexpected viewers of the performance will share their experience with others. In that sense, the performance quickly reaches a crowd that is larger than the physical one assembled on the street.

164
A handful of the best graffiti artists in the country were asked to produce artwork 'live' on the sides and back of trucks in highly visible locations in Sydney. This action was for the launch of the film *8 Mile*, starring Eminem as a troubled yet talented young rapper. Large crowds gathered to watch the artists work, often sitting for hours in the sun. The resulting mobile billboards then drove around for two weeks. *8 Mile* achieved the biggest opening day and the third biggest opening week for any UIP film in Australia. The box office results were proportionally higher than in other countries.

Client **UIP**
Agency **Mediaedge:CIA / Maverick**
Australia 2003

AMPLIFICATION EFFECT
The activity attracted significant publicity in newspapers, magazines and on the radio.

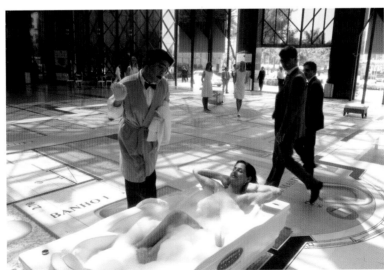

165

To sell apartments in a luxurious condominium in Brazil, a floor plan was printed to scale and laid out in the lobby of one of the main shopping malls in the neighbourhood. Apart from the printed furniture on the plans, real furniture featured in every room, such as an actual bathtub in the bathroom in which a woman took a bath every hour. A performer walked around the apartment, sitting on imaginary chairs and reading invisible newspapers. Genuine estate agents took interested people to visit the actual site. The event was responsible for over 30% of the sales made while it was in place.

Client **Gafisa**
Agency **Publicis Salles Norton**
Brazil 2004

166

Four models walked around
key areas of Singapore's
Central Business District
dressed in a rather peculiar
manner. Their custom-made
suits had daggers fixed to the
back and they carried small
red briefcases explaining the
point of the act.

Client **The Economist**
Agency **Ogilvy & Mather**
Singapore 2004

167

Wishing to convey the urgency
of Nando's tagline 'the craving
has spoken', actors in special
costumes walked around
shopping malls. They proved
that people stopped whatever
they were doing when they
experienced an overwhelming
craving for Nando's, the chain
of chicken restaurants.

Client **Nando's**
Agency **TBWA\Hunt Lascaris**
South Africa 2003

168

A 30-strong team in pyjamas invaded London's financial district to convey the message that British Airways Sleeper Service allows you to get a good night's sleep. They read spoof newspapers promoting the service and started to fall asleep as the day wore on.

Client **British Airways**
Agency **Cunning**
UK 2004

169

The Durex television ad in the UK featured men dressed as sperm getting trapped inside a huge condom. Running concurrently with the ad, sperm men penetrated the streets of London's West End and Soho (the heart of London's sex industry) to protest against Durex. They even tried to get into the most appropriate show in town, *The Vagina Monologues*.

The sperm also appeared on the Dance Floor Chart Club Tour, a collaboration between Durex and the popular MTV dance programme. With 35 live appearances from the sperm men in different countries, it was true to say that they 'came' all over Europe!

Client **SSL International**
Agency **Universal McCann**
UK 2001

170
These noses were running in shopping centres, at traffic intersections during rush hour and on treadmills at gyms to promote the vitamin-C-packed Liquifruit.

Client **Ceres Fruit Juices**
Agency **Network BBDO**
South Africa 2003

171

To launch the Mini convertible
to style leaders, the car was
converted into a stage for
street theatre from which
several spoof plays were
performed to summertime
pavement drinkers. Guided by
mock theatre programmes,
the assembled audience
enjoyed the following film
parodies: *2001: A Space
Odyssey, Frankenstein,
Robinson Crusoe* and
Chariots of Fire.

Client **Mini Cooper**
Agency **Cunning**
UK 2004

172

In the Netherlands, the campaign 'Society, that's you' continuously reminded the Dutch population that it was only possible to achieve a better society when everyone did his or her part. A department store's window displayed the 'little things' that could be done to make society much pleasanter. Models in five cities across the Netherlands acted out these 'little things', such as giving up their seat in the bus.

Client **Sire**
Agency **Lowe**
the Netherlands 2002

AMPLIFICATION EFFECT
National newspapers and news broadcasts responded enthusiastically to the event.

173

At a very busy intersection, a beautiful model paraded around in a provocative outfit, making it impossible for passers-by not to turn and look. Upon looking, people realized they were participating in a promotion for a product to cure a stiff neck. This action put smiles on the faces of both men and their wives or partners.

Client **Recalcine Laboratory**
Agency **TBWA\Frederick**
Chile 2004

174

For the launch of Chicago's Hard Rock Hotel, several local models were hired and dressed in the hotel's lush bathrobes. They were set loose in Chicago's business district during the morning commute, where they stopped people on their way to work, asking: 'Excuse me, can you tell me how to get back to the Hard Rock Hotel?' In less than an hour, word had spread about these unusual hotel guests and local newspaper and television photographers appeared on the scene.

Client **Hard Rock Hotel Chicago**
Agency **Young & Rubicam**
USA 2003

Sensation information conveyed through the senses

We can all confirm that the chances of remembering somebody are much greater if we have touched, smelled, seen, heard or – let's not forget – tasted them in person, rather than just seeing a picture or having a telephone conversation. As Pine and Gilmore state, the more effectively an experience engages the senses, the more memorable it is.[15] **The powerful impact of sensory stimulation applies to everything with which we come into contact.** Freshly baked bread is hard to appreciate without its oven-fresh smell and soft texture. The leather seats (touch), state-of-the-art audio quality (sound), top design (sight) and the smell of newness (smell) make up much of the enjoyment of a new car. It is even possible to buy a spray can of 'new car smell'. Along the same lines, the pleasure that people experience in flying business class is inherently linked to the friendly sound of the airline hostess, the feel of the extended leg room, the taste of a good meal and a glass of champagne.

Companies try to apply this sensory wisdom to their products and services as often as possible. Pine and Gilmore cite the simple example of clever shoeshine operators, 'who augment the smell of polish with crisp snaps of the cloth, scents and sounds that don't make the shoes any shinier but do make the experience more engaging'.[16] In the same vein, companies spend fortunes on research and development to add a heightened sense of taste, feel or smell to their products. In his elaborate study on the topic of sensory marketing, *Brand Sense*, Martin Lindstrom reveals the efforts some major brands will go to. He describes how Kellogg's designs the sound of its product crunching in sound labs, and how Singapore Airlines ensures that the aroma in the cabin is as consistent as the colour scheme, which matches the make-up and uniforms worn by the hostesses.[17]

Traditional advertising, however, is limited in its capacity to convey these rich sensory experiences. How to impart the unique and luxurious sensory pleasures of flying business class on television, even if it is a high-definition plasma screen? A print ad or television commercial can convey a great-tasting cup of coffee, a heavenly bed or an exquisite perfume through clever and imaginative art direction or cinematography. But, even with the best graphics and visuals in the world, other senses remain neglected and the product is not done justice. Moreover, in television commercials or beautifully shot print ads, all products using these media seem to taste as good, smell as delicious, look as nice and feel as soft. Whatever you spend on enhancing the sensory experience of a product, once it has gone through the ruthless filter of traditional advertising its unique difference and thus its persuasiveness is lost. In a highly competitive environment in which all players seem to have similar propositions – the washing powder that best preserves colour, the most sweet-smelling cleaning product, the best-tasting meals, the softest toilet paper, the car radio with the clearest sound – it is a challenge for advertisers to translate the sensory richness and uniqueness of their product to an audience.

Traditional media are aware of their limitations in this regard and try hard to achieve more real-life sensorial experiences. Some media, however, are naturally more flexible. Outdoor media, for example, are much more able to heighten the sensory experience than the medium of radio, which is doomed to a strictly auditory life. **Advertisers, therefore, are constantly in search of non-conventional ways of integrating consumers' senses in their communication.**

Sight

The modern tourist has developed an automatic reflex whenever he or she is confronted with beautiful, breathtaking sights: to bring out their digital cameras or camcorders in an attempt to capture the image for future reference or to share with friends and relatives at home. Yet whether they use photography or video, whether they watch the films at home on a small television set or on a large plasma screen, nothing can beat the live experience. The grandeur and impressive nature of a great landscape can only be appreciated by being there. Two-dimensional simulations do not even come close.

Companies are doing their utmost to provide consumers with first-hand, three-dimensional visual experiences, rather than flat simulations. Areas such as retail marketing and event marketing are by nature much better equipped for this than such traditional media as television and print. Flagship stores turn mundane shopping excursions into visually stunning tours through the world of the brand. The architecture of many corporate buildings is intended

as a visual translation of the company's soul, personality and values, and company tours and factory visits enable corporations to give people a first-hand impression of their brand and products. An extreme example is Volkswagen, who pushed the concept of the factory visit to another level in an attempt to 'make the fascination of automobile production visible to the outside world'. In Germany, the company built a completely transparent factory and invited customers who had bought Phaeton cars to witness several of the vehicle's production stages. What had always happened behind closed doors suddenly became an impressive visual experience.

In advertising, sight is the most dominant of all the senses: almost every campaign or piece of communication somehow appeals to this sense. What follows is a selection of communication efforts that have specifically enhanced or intensified the visual experience.

175

Mounted on a billboard, this three-dimensional light bulb automatically switched on for four seconds whenever a pedestrian passed underneath.

Client **The Economist**
Agency **Abbott Mead Vickers BBDO**
UK 2004

'The challenge on a long-running campaign like *The Economist* is to maintain the momentum and grab people's attention in a different way by introducing new ideas'.

Nigel Roberts, creative director at AMV BBDO in *Contagious Magazine*

176

Shining wider and further than other lights, BMW's Bixenon headlights increase night vision and safety and do not blind oncoming drivers. These benefits were demonstrated in a commercial that showed a BMW, with its headlights on, approaching the audience in a darkened cinema. As the car drew closer, a lighting technician turned up specially positioned lights in the cinema until the whole place was brightly lit, without blinding the audience. When the car's engine was turned off, the lights went down and the cinema was plunged back into darkness.

Client **BMW**
Agency **TBWA\Hunt Lascaris**
South Africa 2003

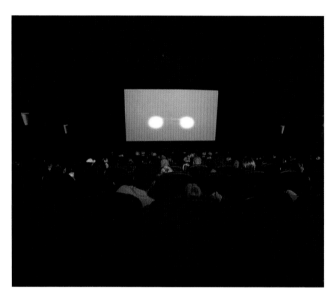

177

This hoarding, 43 metres in length, encouraged passers-by to peak behind the red curtains to satisfy their curiosity, a central theme in the Vanilla Coke campaign. After a week, the curtains were drawn back to reveal the new Vanilla Coke. The visual teaser was combined with extensive sampling.

Client **Coca-Cola**
Agency **Mediaedge:CIA**
Singapore 2003

178

The action for *Time Magazine* wanted people to stand still – in a literal and metaphorical way – on the subject of marriage. These 'peephole' units were built in what appeared to be just another normal construction site fence. However, the same question appeared by all the peepholes: 'Can an amendment really protect the sanctity of marriage?', with a signature from *Time Magazine* below. Passers-by felt compelled to take a look, and behind each hole was a different image.

Client ***Time Magazine***
Agency **Fallon NY**
USA 2005

Sound

Sound is traditionally exploited by television and radio advertising. However, advertising in this form has become background noise, a stream of sound, which is as easy to ignore as it is to listen to. Surprising use of sound can, however, break this pattern and lead to unexpected brand encounters.

179

Who said an advertising billboard can't talk? When the button was pressed, a message ran:

'You'll notice this poster has no printed words. That's because 5 million adult Canadians would have a hard time reading them. But help is available. If you know someone who needs help with reading, writing or math, just look under Learn in the Yellow Pages. This message is brought to you by ABC Canada Literacy Foundation.'

Client **ABC Canada Literacy Foundation**
Agency **Taxi**
Canada 2002

180

Nova – a new radio station on Sydney's crowded airwaves – built a television campaign around the promise 'sounds different'. It suggested that everything in real life sounded different when listening to Nova. The campaign was extended through the use of floor signs, which produced different noises – a phone ringing, a foghorn and a baby screaming – every time someone stepped on them.

Client **DMG**
Agency **Saatchi & Saatchi**
Australia 2003

182

If you are in a bar, the moments you spend in the toilet are often the only silent ones. For advertisers, this means a good time to start a conversation. Bundy Draught, determined to attack the beer market, developed 'talking' ads that were installed in the male washrooms of selected bars. Standard washroom picture frames had movement sensors and speakers attached; each time someone stepped up to the urinal, the girl in the ad would appear to speak directly to them:

'Look that's nothing to be ashamed of. Trust me. That's about average. Average for this place anyway, 'cos they serve Bundy Draught on tap, served at 2 degrees, it makes the Bundy go down extra cold.'

Eight different messages ran in rotation. The main aim of the campaign was to get bars across Australia to stock Bundy Draught. Outstripping all expectations, the product was taken on by 900 bars.

Client **Diageo**
Agency **Mindshare Sydney**
Australia 2004

181

Hewlett-Packard's competition offered one enthusiastic and talented guitarist the chance to win a Fender guitar. Special bus shelters were created that encased real Fender guitars and played music at regular intervals. The sonic posters allowed people to push buttons and hear different guitar solos. By the end of the campaign, though, four Fender guitars had been stolen.

Client **Hewlett-Packard**
Agency **Publicis**
UK 2004

Touch

At Upperdare parties, the erotic version of Tupperware parties, much of the pleasure is derived from the participants touching all sorts of erotic toys and gadgets. It proves that some products just need to be picked up and felt to be fully appreciated. For these products where touch is an essential part of the experience, such as mobile phones or clothing, it is good to look for ways to bring consumers – literally – in touch with the products.

183

In Panama, many people take the bus every day to travel long distances to work, setting off at around 6am and returning 12 hours later. Flex Mattresses placed mini mattresses on bus windows so passengers could rest their heads and snooze until they reached their destination.

Client **Flex Mattresses**
Agency **Insight DDB**
Panama 2004

184

There is no better time to inform consumers of the appeal and comfort of quality toilet paper than at events and festivals where dirty, smelly toilets are generally the norm. Charmin Ultra organized a 'Potty Palooza' tour in the USA, with squeaky-clean, trailer-mounted bathrooms complete with running water, wallpaper, faux wood floors and plenty of Charmin toilet paper. Feedback was instant. The 30 Charmin-sponsored bathrooms had people lining up for 15 to 20 minutes. They reached 2 million consumers at more than 20 events nationwide, including the Super Bowl. Research showed a 14% increase in Charmin sales among those people who used the facilities.

Client **Procter & Gamble**
Agency **Starcom Mediavest**
USA 2003

'It's a category that consumers don't think much about. To break through that and understand the benefits of Charmin Ultra, you really need to try it.'

Diane Cercle, Charmin brand manager

185

Special ink overprinted a
picture of the Touareg to give
the impression that a real layer
of mud covered the car.
The magazine readers were
invited to use the piece of
cotton, on the first page of the
four-page insert, to remove
the mud and unveil the car.

Client **VAG Group**
Agency **Almap BBDO**
Brazil 2004

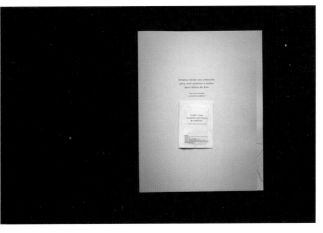
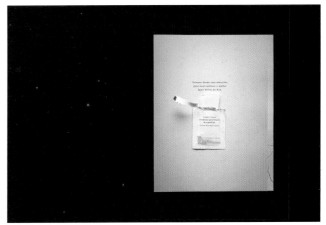
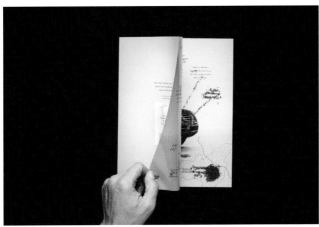
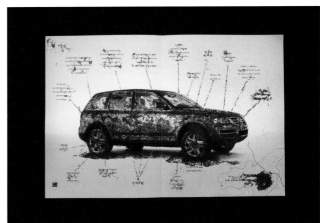
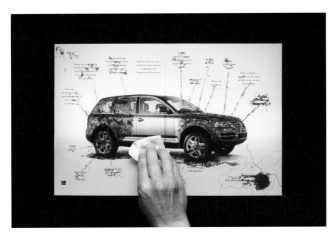

Smell

In Patrick Süskind's novel, *Perfume*, the infant Jean-Baptiste Grenouille is born in the slums of eighteenth-century France possessing one sublime gift: a highly refined sense of smell. Through vivid and detailed descriptions, the author brings to life all the smells experienced by the main character, from oils and herbs to brass doorknobs and fresh-cut wood. Süskind succeeds brilliantly in using literature to tell a story in which the sense of smell plays a crucial role.

Traditional advertising finds itself in much the same position – unable to communicate smell directly – but is less well-equipped to deal with it. We have seen television commercials for coffee or chocolate with people seemingly enraptured by the smell. But a close-up of a swirling coffee aroma around trembling nostrils is not very convincing. It is only upon entering a real coffee shop, for example, that the full appeal of the proposition becomes clear. The challenge for products with captivating smells is to simulate the odour in the absence of the actual product. Perfume ads, for instance, have resolved this issue by adding scent strips to magazines.

In some sectors, such as food and beverages or perfumes and toiletries, the scent is a crucial component of the brand. Yet most of the brands in these sectors revert to media that cannot communicate smells. It is crucial to explore how smells can be communicated in a more complete and direct way. After all, our sense of smell cannot be turned off; it is in the air we breathe and should not be underestimated.[18]

186
Affixed at the eye level of dogs, these billboards had dog food hidden behind them. The odour was released through small holes in the bowl and made the dogs sniff around them. The billboards were placed close to specialist dealers in key urban areas of Germany.

Client **Affinity Petcare**
Agency **Leo Burnett GmbH**
Germany 2004

187

The format of a perfume ad, where a scent sample is added to the page, was used by a brand from a totally different category: Mercedes-Benz. The brand placed diesel smell strips in special-interest magazines for truckers. The ad roused truck drivers' desire for a test-drive and new registrations that year increased by 9.5%.

Client **DaimlerChrysler**
Agency **Scholz & Friends Berlin**
Germany 2004

The new Actros.

For men.

Mercedes-Benz
Berlin · Paris · Mailand · Berlin

188

Cinemas were filled with the sweet aroma of Panettone after a diffusion mechanism was placed in the air-conditioning systems, allowing the audience to experience the same sensations as the characters in the commercial.

Client **Bauducco & CIA**
Agency **Almap BBDO**
Brazil 2003

AMPLIFICATION EFFECT
The project ran in 32 cinemas and created much discussion among members of the public and in the press. The interaction with the public was heightened by the final 7 seconds of the commercial: 'You, there in the movie theatre, you don't have to hug each other. It's just the aroma of Panettone. That's all.'

189

On the first day of spring – traditionally associated with spring-cleaning – Ajax spotlessly cleaned the inside of a Prague tram and decorated it with fresh flowers, as a perfect demonstration of its fresh fragrance and cleaning efficacy. The outside of the tram was branded with the Ajax colours. Ajax funding also meant that everyone could use that tram route free of charge.

Client **Colgate Palmolive**
Agency **Mediaedge:CIA**
The Czech Republic 2001

AMPLIFICATION EFFECT
The event generated a huge amount of free publicity coverage not only in Prague but also in nationwide media.

Taste

Sight, sound, touch and even smell can be reproduced in some form in the absence of the actual product. Taste cannot. The sound of wine being poured into a glass, its deep red colour and its rich aroma can all be simulated, but it is impossible to reproduce its unique taste. To know what something tastes like, we have to taste it.

Samplings and tastings are an unavoidable step along the path of acceptance for any new food item or beverage launched on the market, especially when the product's taste is different, special or new. When Senseo, the new coffee system by Philips and Sara Lee, was launched throughout Europe, one of the challenges was to convince people that the coffee actually had a different taste. Extensive tastings in supermarkets attributed greatly to Senseo's successful market introduction.

While taste may be the toughest nut to crack for conventional media, it is the easiest sense to link to a service or product, according to Pine and Gilmore. They claim that it is possible 'to add taste sensations simply by serving food and drink'[19]. It is the strategy adopted by hair saloons, where a cup of coffee is offered while you are being treated. The same tactic would be appreciated in any situation where people have to wait: in banks, post offices or retail stores.

190

To convince people that the new Canderel sugar had superb taste, the product was linked to an altogether accepted delicacy: fresh strawberries. A strawberry field was installed on a huge plaza in Paris, where people could pick strawberries and dip them in the new Canderel powder product, experiencing for themselves that new Canderel had a superb taste.

The event attracted 24,000 people in 4 days, in spite of an unexpected metro strike. Apart from convincing 65% of visitors that Canderel tasted better than expected, the biggest sign of success was that the neighbouring hypermarket sold 5 times as much Canderel in the two weeks following the event.

Client **Canderel**
Agency **Mediaedge:CIA**
France 2003

AMPLIFICATION EFFECT
Posters and leaflets publicized the event locally and were part of a larger campaign that included posters and advertising in women's magazines. The strawberry field received tremendous press coverage in women's magazines and was a feature story on the television news.

191

To announce the red, limited-edition Senseo coffee, five bus shelters were transformed into temporary free coffee stations. Instead of staring at the usual ad posters, passengers were treated to a real cup of Senseo coffee. While bus drivers were initially grumpy about the disruption, they soon informed each other where the coffee was on offer.

Advertiser **Philips**
the Netherlands 2004

Interaction any communication in which the consumer is actively involved

Brands are like people: they have a personality, a way of behaving and a set of values. Relationships between people and brands are often compared to relationships between people. They deal with the same issues of trust and loyalty; they go from wild flings to long-term commitments. If we accept this, then we must also acknowledge that many brands handle relationships in a strange way. Do you have any relationships in which the other person never lets you speak, intervenes in your life when it best suits him or her and never meets you face to face? I would guess not, as it would not be much of a relationship. Yet the traditional advertising model is still built on a one-way push that force-feeds messages to the public. These messages are created behind closed doors and leave little room for consumers to contribute. The public may be entertained, may pass opinion on it, but their reactions will not change the transmitted message.

Non-interactive communication is comparable with a rehearsed and prepared music concert, to which the consumer can only listen. Interactive communication, on the other hand, is a concert where the order and content is co-determined by the public, and where the public can sometimes even go on stage. Interactive communication is more like a karaoke club and less like a classical concerto. The sender-receiver paradigm is transcended and the consumer becomes actively involved in the communication. **Without the consumer's input, interactive communication is an unfinished product.**

There are 1001 ways of creating interactivity: large-scale events, competitions and contests of all kinds, promotional tours, conferences and conventions, incentives, interactive games, interactive television and opinion polls, among others. **The great advantage of interactive communication is that it is much more memorable than passive exposure to a one-way information transfer**. Actions go much further than words. People are also much more likely to share an actual experience with others. Interactions ingrain themselves in the consumer's consciousness.

Interactions are the best way to overcome consumer cynicism. **Brands that hide behind the safe façade of traditional advertising become a sitting duck.** It is much easier to criticize someone you have not met in person. Only when brands face consumers full on and interact with them, do they present themselves as open and direct. As a consequence, consumers are less severe in their judgment. This is why politicians are so keen to meet personally as many voters as possible during an election campaign. As in human relationships, constant interaction is the key to keeping a brand-consumer relationship alive and fresh.

As a technique, interaction differs from sensation in the way it involves consumers. Sensations activate the senses, but remain passive experiences, while interactions are the result of active participation on the consumer's part. There are two types of interaction, which have different levels of commitment: the consumer as participant and the consumer as co-creator. In the former, the consumer is allowed on the stage to play the instruments; in the latter, the consumer helps to build the stage and to determine which instruments appear.

Consumer as participant

One of the reasons we are so fond of theme parks is that they allow us to enjoy fully the experience in the role of participant, without having to worry about anything else. Everything is prepared and set up for us to come in and have the time of our life. This clear line between those who organize and stage the experience and those who participate in it applies to most branded events or experiences. **As a participant, we experience what other people have designed for us to experience.** In much the same way, event organizers, game developers or brand managers determine what kind of experience needs to be created, what kind of thrill or exhilaration should be the result of the interaction.

Staged interactions take the participants on a guided, interactive tour through the world of the brand. While brands give the audience the chance to interact with them, they retain complete control over the experience.

'With this generation, it's, "I know you're marketing something to me, and you know I know, so if you want me to try a new chicken sandwich, that's cool – just give me some crazy chicken to boss around".'

Alex Bogusky in *Wired Magazine*

192

Something strange appeared on the Web in April 2004: a chicken dressed in garters that obeyed every command viewers gave. The Subservient Chicken site's technology allowed users to type in almost anything and watch the chicken respond. He could break-dance, take part in a pillow fight, do karate or kung fu and smoke a cigarette. Within a day of its release, the site had received a million hits; within a week, the figure had risen to 20 million. A year later, the site had totalled 396 million hits and about 14 million unique visitors.

The Subservient Chicken campaign was slated for failing to push the product, but that was the point. 'There's a huge lure to obscurity,' explains David Art Wales of the New York consulting firm Ministry of Culture, 'That's one of the keys – giving people something to discover – which is the antithesis of the way most advertising works.'

Client **Burger King**
Agency **Crispin Porter + Bogusky**
USA 2004

 AMPLIFICATION EFFECT
Since branding on the site was subtle, questions arose as to who was behind the initiative. Any doubt about the connection with Burger King ended when mention of the Subservient Chicken website appeared in Burger King television commercials.

From press to mobile

For the first time in Austria a traditional media (newspaper) and a new media (MMS) were linked to establish a new type of media experience

Objective:
Strengthen the image of A1, increase awareness and encourage trial of the new service MMS (mobile-image-sending-service).

Idea:
National newspaper DER STANDARD is published without press photos and with an explanation how to get them via MMS on the mobile phone.

Strategy:
Promote the innovative service MMS by using a classical mass media in the most spectacular and dramatic way.

Results:
51,3% (!) of enabled readers downloaded these press photos onto their mobile phones. This outstanding idea immediately became the talk of the town and thus generated a lot of extra press coverage in other national and even international media.

Why was this special:
The first time ever a daily newspaper was published without press photos. In this cooperation a traditional media and the new media were linked to establish a new type of media experience.

193

On 25 January 2003, Austria's national newspaper, *Der Standard*, was published without photos. Instead, readers were confronted with empty picture boxes and instructions on how to receive the missing photos on their mobile. This collaboration between old and new media provided people with the opportunity to experience Multimedia Messaging System (MMS). Of the readers armed with this technology, 51.3% of them downloaded the photos; for those not equipped with MMS technology, the missing pictures were printed on the inside pages of the newspaper.

Client **Mobilkom Austria**
Agency **Saatchi & Saatchi**
Austria 2003

AMPLIFICATION EFFECT
This interactive mechanism generated a lot of extra press coverage in both national and international media.

194

Doors to go (and try at home)! That is what the text on these posters proclaimed. Swedoor showed its range of front doors full-size on a giant swatch so people could pull off a printed sample and see how good the door looked at home before buying it.

Client **Swedoor**
Agency **ANR BBDO**
Sweden 1999

195

If home delivery works for pizzas, why shouldn't it work for housing loans? This is what web-based SBAB must have thought when they sent out housing-loan advisors on scooters. All customers had to do was call a telephone number and the advisor rode over to their home with a laptop to offer instant mortgage help. It gave many of the SBAB staff an opportunity to meet new customers face to face.

Client **SBAB**
Agency **TBWA\Stockholm**
Sweden 2004

196

Web-based housing-loans company SBAB turned ordinary advertising boards into small offices to get directly in touch with potential clients. Inside, handling officers from SBAB had laptop computers and were ready to answer any questions about housing loans. The text on the three sides of the offices read: 'Transfer your housing loan with me', 'Leave your bank here' and 'Get a lower interest rate here'.

Client **SBAB**
Agency **TBWA\Stockholm**
Sweden 2002

197

Pie maker Fray Bentos
organized a contest entitled
'The Real Bloke Challenge'
to connect with its male target
audience. The first phase was
a road show, which arrived in
10 major cities around the UK
and encouraged punters to
take part in various challenges,
sample the product and enter
themselves for the 'Real Bloke'
competition. In a second
phase, finalists from each city
were photographed and printed
on 6 sheet posters that carried
a phone number for the public
to vote for their favourite.

Client **Campbell**
Agency **Naked
Communications**
UK 2003

AMPLIFICATION EFFECT
The road show was promoted
locally through posters and
radio partnerships. Local press
took up the campaign, running
stories with headlines like 'Pie
Idol', while the national final
gained significant coverage in
the national tabloids.

198

For cat-food brands, cats are as much a part of the target group as their owners. Meow Mix opened a temporary restaurant (also known in advertising terms as a pop-up or guerrilla store) in the heart of Manhattan with the first-ever menu with dishes for patrons of the two- and four-legged variety. While cats dined on Fillet Meow (beef in gravy), their owners enjoyed tenderloin of beef with horseradish sauce in a baguette. As well as the obligatory gift shop, there was also a game area where visitors could play cat-themed games like 'Feeding Time' and 'Hairball Toss'.

Client **The Meow Mix Company**
Agency **Grand Central Terminal**
USA 2004

AMPLIFICATION EFFECT
Eartha Kitt, who played Catwoman in the Batman television series in the 1960s, attended the grand opening. Stories about the restaurant appeared in print and on television all over the world, including NBC News, CNN and *The New York Times*. The Meow Mix restaurant generated more than US $100 million of media coverage in August 2004.

'Cats are such a key part of so many people's lives, yet there are very few public places that are cat friendly.'

Richard Thompson, CEO The Meow Mix Company

199

Custom-made bus-shelters
invited passers-by to be DJs
for a brief moment. When
people spun the record on the
left, they heard the 'I'm lovin'
it' brand song. The copy then
told them to spin the record on
the right, at which point they
heard scratch sounds added to
the original music at intervals.

Client **McDonald's**
Agency **OMD**
China 2003

200

Nike's Battlegrounds campaign
provided the perfect platform
for the global sports brand to
interact at grass-roots level
with its core audience. A series
of one-on-one streetball
competitions were guided
by simple rules: anyone could
play but at the end of the
competition, only one person
could be 'The Boss'. Around the
world, hundreds of contestants
competed against each other
wherever there was a flat
surface and a hoop. The
big finale was played on a
spectacular set. The basketball
half-court was surrounded by
a tall cage at the top of which
flames appeared at intervals.
Every time a player scored, the
flames shot up.

Advertiser **Nike**
USA, Italy, Germany, France,
Spain 2004

AMPLIFICATION EFFECT
The competition was turned
into a television show, which
aired on MTV.

201

As an act of social responsibility, Smirnoff organized a taxi service at bars, offering people in different stages of inebriation a free ride home. Taxi Smirnoff, as it was called, was announced with the clear message: 'If you drink, get a taxi. Save your money and your life.'

Client **Smirnoff**
Agency **Bullet**
Brazil 2003

AMPLIFICATION EFFECT
The taxi was promoted in bars on napkins and glasses and in the toilets. Messages were adapted to their specific locations. A clip on a glass read: 'If you don't wanna go home alone, call me: 3257 4775', while a sticker on a mirror carried the message: 'How many fingers in here? If you're not sure, get a taxi.'

202

In Reebok's 'Escape the Sofa' commercial, a lazy couch potato is driven out of his house by a living and breathing sofa. Sofa Games, a series of city-based street sports and lifestyle events, brought this creative platform to life.

Client **Reebok**
Agency **Naked Communications**
UK 2001

AMPLIFICATION EFFECT
Entry to each Sofa Game was secured through a dedicated website. People were directed to the site through a range of unconventional outdoor media, such as real sofas in prominent city locations, which had been spray-painted with the URL or a fully functioning motorized sofa that drove around city centres.

Local shoe retailers were given custom-made merchandise linked to the event to give away with Reebok purchases, which acted as an incentive for the stores to maximize their sales on the back of the event.

203

Chocolat Jacques is a famous Belgian chocolate brand with a medieval knight as its icon. To announce its merger with another important Belgian chocolate brand called Callebaut, a wedding was organized between Knight Jacques and Princess Callebaut in Belgium's biggest cathedral. Interaction with the public was further encouraged through a competition: all couples that showed up in their wedding outfit had the chance of winning a honeymoon.

Client **Chocolat Jacques**
Agency **mortierbrigade**
Belgium 2005

AMPLIFICATION EFFECT
The wedding and the competition were announced on national radio and billboards. Real wedding invitations were also distributed. The event received huge coverage in the national media, and more than 3,000 people attended the wedding.

204

The popular Tango Apple television ad, in which young men get 'the hit of the whole fruit', was an ideal campaign to bring to life. The result was the Tango Apple Big Drench Tour, which was composed of various elements.

Apple Roulette invited people to have a full-on Tango Apple drenching. By pulling a cord inside a specially built chamber, you had a 1 in 25 chance of getting the Apple Drench experience.

Armed with super soakers, kids could drench each other in certain alleys and side streets that had been turned into super-soaker war zones with a specially built urban obstacle course. The aim of the game was to get the most drenched.

Research showed that one week after the event, 32% of the participants had bought Tango Apple, of which 25% were infrequent or non-drinkers. There was a significant shift in Tango Apple sales during the event period.

Client **Tango**
Agency **Cunning**
UK 2003

AMPLIFICATION EFFECT
The event was communicated through various media: television, radio, flyposters, the Internet and street signs.

205

Outside the main gates of the
Big Day Out, New Zealand's
largest outdoor music festival,
a girl pretending to have just
been dumped invited girls to
smash her ex's car with a
sledgehammer. This simple idea
to draw attention to *nzgirl*,
an online magazine for girls,
generated much word of mouth
during and after the festival.

Client *nzgirl*
Agency **DDB New Zealand**
New Zealand 2005

206

To promote the PlayStation
version of the Olympic Games,
people were invited to break
Olympic records, such as
weight lifting, on the streets.

Client **PlayStation**
Agency **TBWA\Today**
the Netherlands 2004

207

As official sponsor of athletics in the UK, Norwich Union started a campaign to encourage more children to participate in sporting activity to fight obesity. Rather than passively communicating this ambition, the insurance company also offered the means to make it happen. They transformed London's Trafalgar Square into an athletics course where children competed in a whole range of events.

Client **Norwich Union**
Agency **Mediaedge:CIA**
UK 2004

Consumer as co-creator

Unless consumers have a final say in the content of an experiential platform, they continue to think in terms of 'them' versus 'us', no matter how fun, inclusive or memorable the experience is. This divide disappears when consumers become co-creators and help to determine the rules and content of the interaction. Then, at best, it becomes unclear who leads who or who gets the most out of the interaction. It simply becomes a shared experience. Brand and consumers 'are in it together'. For a brand, this is a very desirable position to be in.

Today, it is not unusual for consumers to invent a brand's new advertising campaign, baseline or packaging design, with or without guidance and permission from the companies involved. Sometimes, consumers are even invited to co-create new products and services. These kinds of interactions, also known as consumer-generated content, can produce win-win situations for brands and consumers. For consumers, it presents an opportunity to become involved in the creative process and enter a zone that was previously the exclusive terrain of creative agencies and brand managers. For brands, by promoting consumers to co-creators, they attain a higher level of complicity with the consumer. It is the difference between organizing your own party with friends and going to somebody else's party. One is not necessarily more fun than the other, but the experience is different. If you and your friends throw a party, the experience starts much earlier – brainstorming sessions, guest lists, organizing catering. If the party is a success this is reward enough for all the efforts that you have put into it as a group. Showing up at somebody else's party on the day itself can never – no matter how fun – reach the same level of complicity. The journey and the end result are of equal importance in the experience. By involving the consumer in the whole creative process, the length of his or her experience is prolonged.

Co-creation can be an answer to the anaemia that brands are confronted with. 'Tapping into the collective intellectual capital of consumers yields great creative and "real" content,' according to the online firm trendwatching.com. It goes on to suggest that co-creation is very much in touch with today's empowered and mature consumers, who also have the means to be creative and express themselves (from digital photography to online tools and software). Central is the urge for a sense of control. Trendwatching.com states that today's consumers 'create their own playgrounds, their own comfort zones, their own universe. It's the empowered and better informed and switched on consumer.'[20] Apart from offering companies fresh and invigorated input, the transfer of power to consumers might also be the most noble thing that brands can do today. Gavin MacDonald draws an analogy with the Roman Empire: 'As the Roman tyrant would demonstrate his magnanimity by handing power over the gladiator's life to the crowd, so canny brands today hand key elements of decision making over to consumers – or appear to.'[21]

Rather than forcing the completed brand image onto consumers, brands can portray themselves as being more open and generous by allowing consumers to fill in the gaps and express their vision. As Chris Aldhous, European creative director for Hewlett-Packard at Publicis London, commented on the HYPE Gallery campaign (see campaign 208, opposite): 'We were at the mercy of what they created. The quality of the communication message relied on the quality of the work they contributed....We surrender control to the audience.'[22] By choosing to go down this path, brands finally accept that they are no longer and never have been in full control of their image.

208

Hewlett-Packard wanted to promote HP digital imaging, printing and projecting equipment to the next generation of artists, photographers and film-makers. Based on the knowledge that the creative mind wants to put what is in their head onto paper and in front of other people, an art gallery was founded to encourage young creatives to show their work using HP technology.

Artists were invited to turn up with an original digital picture or short film on disk that was inspired by a word or phrase containing the letters

H and P. Pictures were run out on HP printers and exhibited. Films were shown on HP projectors in the 'HYPE film bunker'. There were 1,193 pieces of printed artwork and 94 films submitted to the gallery, which had 4,000 visitors. The success of the London gallery inspired HP to repeat the project in Paris, Moscow, Singapore and Milan the following year.

Client **Hewlett-Packard**
Agency **Publicis**
UK 2004

'The unique idea about the gallery was that nothing was in the gallery until the opening night. People walked in and all they got was a huge white space.'

Belinda Parmar, senior planner for Hewlett-Packard

AMPLIFICATION EFFECT
An ad campaign was conceived and executed in the same spirit as the gallery itself, using artists' work on postcards, press and cinema ads. Once the gallery reached capacity, it was uploaded to hypegallery.com, which perfectly resembled the experience inside the gallery. The site also gave artists from around the world the opportunity to upload work. The site received 5.5 million hits and 2,700 works of art were uploaded. The gallery continues to accept art and films and has evolved into the world's biggest interactive online art gallery.

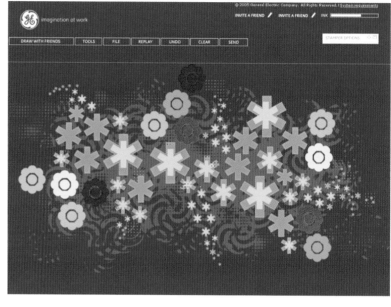

209

For many people, the easiest way to explain a complex idea to others is to pick up a pad and pencil and sketch it out. General Electric made this possible online. As part of their Imagination at Work marketing strategy, they launched a pen program that allowed people to interact and brainstorm through online drawings.

Through a deceptively simple interface – www.imaginationcubed.com – people were invited to draw whatever they wished on a clean white canvas using their mouse as a pen. In true co-creator fashion, this campaign did not put forward any content. It simply gave an online community the means to sketch their ideas and interact, and by so doing it brought a whole new dimension to online idea generation.

The original version of the site was intended for solo brainstorming, but the second generation, launched in 2004, empowered people to collaborate and share ideas. For the initial release in 2003, users from 140 countries emailed 6 million sketches to 1.5 million recipients.

Client **General Electric**
Agency **Atmosphere BBDO**
USA 2004

'[This campaign] provides consumers with a large enough sandbox for two or three like-minded people to play in, with a host of shovels, buckets, shapes and tools to demonstrate their "Imagination at work".'

Joseph Jaffe, www.imediaconnection.com /content/6096.asp

210

CokeLAB, Coca-Cola's sub-brand for nightlife in Belgium, invited their target audience of youngsters and clubbers to come up with new and surprising party concepts. The contest went a step further than picking their brains. The team with the best idea received 25,000 euros to make their dream party reality with the help of a professional event agency.

Client **Coca-Cola**
Agency **Demonstrate**
Belgium 2004

AMPLIFICATION EFFECT
People were recruited through a print and television campaign and through a mailing to the addresses on the databases of leading nightclubs.

The struggles, frustrations and hopes of the teams were filmed and broadcast in the CokeLAB television programme *Create Your Night.*

CREATE YOUR NIGHT
AND WE'LL MAKE IT HAPPEN!

COCA-COLA ZOEKT EEN TEAM VAN TWEE TOT VIER VRIENDEN TUSSEN 18 EN 26 JAAR OM EEN ONWAARSCHIJNLIJK FEESTJE TE BOUWEN!

Denk je 'Dat zie ik wel zitten!', surf dan als de bliksem naar **www.CokeLAB.be** en vat je party-project in enkele lijnen samen. Coca-Cola en een gespecialiseerde nightlife jury belonen de origineelste ideeën!

De enige voorwaarde is dat je zin hebt om:

• de nacht van je dromen te organise-ren! (Kom voor de dag met een origi-nele locatie, je favoriete muziek, een bijzonder decor en funky

thema zonder je zorgen te maken over het prijskaartje want je wordt gesteund door een professioneel team.)

• al je vrienden uit te nodigen en honder-den andere coolcats.

• in het middelpunt van de belangstel-ling te staan.

• gefilmd te worden tijdens de hele voorbereiding en je partyconcept op televisie te zien schitteren!

Create Your Night. Create Your Party!
Meer info? www.CokeLAB.be

JIM

CREATE YOUR NIGHT
Coke LAB

Stunt a difficult, unusual or dangerous feat

In 1969 John Lennon and Yoko Ono started a campaign with the goal of putting 'world peace' on the map. It ran for a year and became known as the 'Year for Peace'. Although the campaign included press conferences and billboards, it is something of an entirely different nature that made it famous. On 26 May 1969 John and Yoko moved into room 1742 of the Queen Elizabeth Hotel in Montreal, Canada. For seven days, they talked Peace from the comfort of their own bed to anyone who would listen. Unsurprisingly the whole world listened. Several cultural icons of the day, among them Tommy Smothers, Timothy Leary, Dick Gregory and, most famously, right-wing hawk Al Capp came to join the discussion. The event culminated in the classic live bedroom recording of 'Give Peace a Chance'.

The Montreal bed session proved to be a most successful publicity stunt. It generated huge media coverage: the American television channel CBC not only recorded the interviews, but also paid to fly most of the famous guests to the bedside. In other words, the media was responsible for turning the event into what it was.

The Lennon and Ono example shows how closely publicity stunts are linked with and in need of media coverage. While for most of the campaigns featured in this book, additional coverage in local or national media is a cherry on the cake, **most stunts are designed with the specific purpose of gaining free publicity**. Without it, they would be nothing more than isolated events carried out in front of the eyes of a few.

The feverish search for media coverage is easy to explain. First, news content delivered directly by media channels has less chance of being filtered out by the public than standard advertising messages. While traditional advertising content is biased by nature, news content at least has some degree of objectivity. Second, it is free publicity, unpaid coverage of a brand and, therefore, a perfect way to get maximum return on a small investment.

Obtaining media coverage, however, requires an understanding of the weak spots of the so-called gatekeepers, the people who decide what is news and what is not. One of these weak spots is the media's love of the original and the remarkable. In his book on spectacular publicity stunts, Mark Borkowski states that it is about 'setting up situations that are so intriguing and so bizarre that they are irresistible to the press'.[23] Yoko and John understood that – a famous couple protesting in their pyjamas is not something you see

every day. Emanuel Rosen observed much the same in *The Anatomy of Buzz* when he stated that 'outrageous stimuli create buzz'[24], an observation that is as much valid for all of us as it is for the media.

Another crucial element in making sure the media picks up a story is imagery. A picture tells a thousand words, as the saying goes, and in media terms that is quite some money. Images condense all dramatic elements around a theme into one striking visual that invites the viewer to read about it. **In terms of PR, imagery is the easy way into a story, making even the least accessible and most difficult stories attractive to a wide group of people.** Protest groups such as Greenpeace are experts in setting up visually attractive stunts that tell their story in a glance. The image of their small rubber boats at the foot of the great U.S.S. Eisenhower Steams in 1988 provided the perfect visual metaphor for their David and Goliath battle against nuclear testing. The more complex or unattractive the story, the more important it is to try and speak the visual language that everyone understands.

Of course, brands want as much return as possible from any free publicity they generate. The golden rule is that good stunts must be a gigantic extrapolation of the core of the brand. Matthew Freud, founder of the company Freud Communications, underlines the dangers of a stunt that is nothing more than random noisemaking: 'As a standalone marketing discipline, PR can be very dangerous. You can raise the volume level to 11, but if you have very little to say you will be caught in a slightly embarrassing silence.'[25] **Stunts should always be an outrageous, yet truthful articulation of what the brand is about.**

The above-mentioned rough-and-ready rules for stunts will take you far: think outrageously, think visually and always keep the brand message in mind. There are countless ways to stick to these rules and to turn a brand story into a publicity stunt. Sergio Zyman advises that it is very important 'to take advantage of every natural opportunity to get publicity for your brand. If there's something you want people to know about and you don't have a natural opportunity, make one up.' He gives an example aimed at the owner of a small pizza place: 'You could announce that you're going to try to set the world record for the biggest pizza. Invite the high-school football team to roll out the dough and have the kids in a nearby kindergarten smear sauce on it.'[26] This way of thinking is feasible for any kind of business. In terms of the publicity stunt, the sky is the limit.

Larger than life

There is no reason to be falsely modest about your product or brand.
On the contrary, if you honestly believe that the world should know
about you, it will serve you well to make it seem as big and as
awesome as possible. Forget conventional ideas of reality; create
a unique, larger-than-life reality.

211

The figure of Richard Branson
is so seamlessly integrated with
the Virgin brand that whenever
he receives publicity – whether
it is by ballooning over the
ocean, spraying champagne on
new Virgin flight attendants at a
graduation ceremony or flying
into India wearing a bright,
virgin-red Bhangra outfit – so
does Virgin. For the USA launch
of Virgin Cola in May 1998, he
drove a vintage World War II
tank into New York's Times
Square, demolishing a wall of
Coca-Cola cans. A similar stunt
was later carried out in Brussels
using a bulldozer.

Advertiser **Virgin Cola**
USA 1998

AMPLIFICATION EFFECT
The stunt ensured that Virgin
Cola appeared on the front
of every major newspaper in
the country.

'When Richard Branson
sends out a press release
claiming that he's going
to drive a tank through
Manhattan to introduce
Virgin Cola, he's showing
us that he's a guy who
doesn't play by the same
rules as Coke and Pepsi
and that he's going to
fight them head on.'

Sergio Zyman in *The End of
Advertising As We Know It*

AMPLIFICATION EFFECT
The stunt received extensive coverage. During the tour, hundreds of thousands of business cards were handed out telling people to go to www.miniusa.com.

212

In the run-up to the weekend, Mini saw an opportunity to inspire people about their weekend activities and, in the process, position the new Mini as the anti sport utility vehicle (SUV). A 2,600-pound Mini was placed on a specially built roof rack of a Ford Excursion, the extra-large SUV, with a sign that read: 'What are you doing for fun this weekend?'

Client **Mini Cooper**
Agency **Crispin Porter + Bogusky**
USA 2002

'It really stopped the traffic every time we drove it around'

Jack Pitney, general manager Mini USA

213

Vertically parked cars carried the message: 'Wouldn't it have been better if you'd left the car at home?'. Taking place one week before the European Day without Cars, this stunt stressed some people's unnecessary use of cars.

Client **Town Hall of Madrid**
Agency **Saatchi & Saatchi**
Spain 2002

214

To illustrate its climbing ability
and fulfil the campaign slogan
'Go anywhere and do anything',
a Jeep Grand Cherokee
ascended all thirty stories of
Two Penn Plaza in New York
to reach its VIP – Vertically
Inclined Parking – space. Once
parked vertically at the top
of the building's east side, it
remained there throughout the
day. A film of the stunt could
be viewed online.

Advertiser **DaimlerChrysler**
USA 2004

'The raining men
campaign was the best
idea I have ever had
the privilege of seeing
come to life. Ideas like
this don't come around
very often.'

Sophie Baker, brand manager *Cleo*

215

Knowing that single girls are looking for cute guys of their own, Ken dolls were attached to 10,000 large clear helium balloons and released at strategic locations over Sydney and Melbourne. It was literally raining men! The stunt was designed for *Cleo*'s 'Bachelor of the Year' promotion.

Client *Cleo*
Agency **Maverick**
Australia 2002

AMPLIFICATION EFFECT
Radio activity was designed around the promotion; for instance, the first 5 balloons taken to the radio studio won VIP invitations to the event.

216

The UK arrival of the Pokemon game was given a touch of drama through a highly visual stunt. The games were transported in large Pokemon-branded trucks accompanied by actors dressed as secret agents, as if the crown jewels themselves were being moved.

Client **Nintendo**
Agency **Cake**
UK 1999

AMPLIFICATION EFFECT
The picture of the Pokemon trucks on board the ship appeared in several newspapers.

217

For the 2003 Rugby World
Cup in Australia, Vodafone
wanted to pull out all the stops
to create awareness over its
long-term sponsorship of
the Australian rugby team.
The largest barge in the
southern hemisphere (110m
long) was constructed to hold
the world's first floating rugby
field. Furthermore, inflatable
replicas of players, as tall
as 5-storey buildings, were
erected at airports (when
supporters flew into each city),
in the immediate vicinity
of the scheduled games and
along dense traffic routes.

Client **Vodafone**
Agency **Maverick**
Australia 2003

AMPLIFICATION EFFECT
The stunt generated enormous
buzz and word of mouth as
well as free publicity in the
extensive newspaper, radio
and television coverage
(metropolitan, national
and international).

Exceptional physical acts

Extreme physical performances capture our imagination because they confront us with the limits of our own abilities. They are therefore great breeding grounds for remarkable communication initiatives.

218

Housing-loans company SBAB challenged the big banks – for real. On the launch of the SBAB cut in interest rates, Christer Malm, managing director of SBAB, gave banks four days to follow the SBAB lead. If they did so, he promised to eat his hat.

Client **SBAB**
Agency **TBWA\Stockholm**
Sweden 2004

AMPLIFICATION EFFECT
In spite of the print ads, television ads, banners, billboards and personal letters to the managing directors of each bank, none of the banks responded in time. The challenge received extensive media coverage. In Stockholm, an event was organized at which Christer Malm ate soup and not his hat as a playful allusion to the daring challenge.

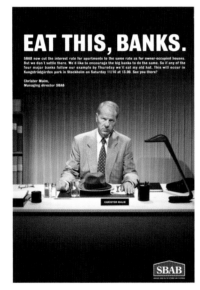

219 & 220

Two billboard stunts defied all laws of gravity and demonstrated the goal Adidas shares with athletes: the desire to surpass limits.

For the first time in history, the game of football was taken to death-defying heights. Two players and a ball were suspended by ropes ten stories above the ground and at a 90-degree angle to the 'pitch'.

Client **Adidas**
Agency **TBWA\Japan**
Japan 2003

AMPLIFICATION EFFECT
Both campaigns attracted a huge amount of publicity worldwide, more specifically, $150 million worth of free publicity for the footballers and $50 million to date for the sprinters.

'Today, I think this is the most impressive example of Talk Value®'

Bob Scarpelli, chairman DDB Chicago, in *Contagious Magazine*

Athletes competed to be the fastest to scale a 100-metre vertical track up the side of a building. The event was timed to coincide with the summer Olympics in Athens. John Merrifield, creative director at TBWA\Japan, refers to the event as 'a 100m dash with a difference'.

Client **Adidas**
Agency **TBWA\Japan**
Japan \ Hong Kong 2004

221

To raise funds and awareness about the challenges faced every day by millions of Canadians with disabilities, the Canadian Foundation for Physically Disabled Persons took disability to new heights. Six-time Paralympic champion Jeff Adams made history by climbing all 1776 stairs of the CN Tower in Toronto, the world's tallest freestanding structure, in a specially designed wheelchair. He raised $100 per step and collected a total of $177,600.

To encourage able-bodied people to think about the need for escalators and ramps for the disabled, provocative messages were stencilled on the subway stairs leading up to the CN Tower.

Client **Foundation for Physically Disabled Persons**
Agency **DDB Toronto**
Canada 2003

AMPLIFICATION EFFECT
Adams's arduous climb was promoted on a 30-second television commercial that featured him training for his ascent, and directed viewers to a website, www.stepuptochange.com, where they could sponsor him. Newspaper, bus shelter and washroom ads put a realistic spin on Adams's heroic climb. Emphasizing the awesome scale of the task, the print ads featured three upward-looking views from the base of the tower.

Breaking records

Breaking existing records or setting new ones is not only a powerful human incentive but it also attracts much media coverage.

222

The promotion team for *Blue Crush*, an American surfing movie, wanted to convert Australian surfing fans into advocates of the film. To involve and engage the surfing crowd, a world record attempt to have the largest number of surfers ride a single wave was set up. The result won the surfers an entry in *The Guinness Book of Records* and the film huge press and radio publicity and a successful film opening.

Client **UIP**
Agency **Mediaedge:CIA/ Maverick**
Australia 2002

AMPLIFICATION EFFECT
To publicize the event and to attract participants, posters were hung in surf shops and large mobile billboards were parked at the beach.

Using a hot news topic, iconic person or well-known place

Rather than inventing ways to get a brand in the news, an easier option is to attach the brand to topics or events that are already newsworthy. Linking a stunt to a hot news topic, a famous person or a well-known location can provide the extra push needed to make headlines.

Actual news topics that are already the focus of the press can be a good platform for any stunt. In their plea for 'under the radar' advertising, Jonathan Bond and Richard Kirshenbaum already pointed out that 'since certain issues and events are on consumers' minds already, you can get a free escort through the radar by connecting with the day's news'.[27]

In a similar vein, people are fascinated by and talk about famous people. Being in the company of celebrities or involving them in a stunt gives access to their fame.

Choosing a famous background for a stunt can also prove crucial. If you decided to go naked with the aim of attracting attention, it would be sensible to do so in a well-known square or near a famous landmark as it would double your chances of being noticed.

223

As a fun and visual way to show off their Christmas stock to the younger generation, Virgin Megastore organized a special class for Santas, which taught them about the changing needs of children. The participating Santas learned about the Nintendo Game Boy Advance – at that time top of many children's wish lists – DVDs and MP3s. To further bridge the generation gap, they were even supplied with a dictionary of kids' slang.

Client **Virgin Records**
Agency **Cake**
UK 2001

224

Not many events have as high a turnout as the national elections. In May 2003, the Belgians voted for the party of their choice. Virgin Express airline made maximum use of this newsworthy event by organizing a special action: the first 1,500 people who cast their vote in a bikini or swimming trunks and sent in a picture of it, received a free return flight to Palma de Mallorca or Bordeaux, two destinations that needed a push at the time. The sender of the most original picture won free flights for a year.

Over 2,500 Belgians bravely took part and the campaign was widely covered in the national press the day after the elections. All pictures could be viewed online.

Client **Virgin Express**
Agency **Duval Guillaume Antwerp**
Belgium 2003

AMPLIFICATION EFFECT
The action was announced in a print and radio campaign.

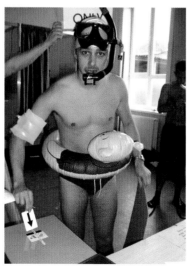

225

As all American eyes turned to the sky for Mir's return to earth on 20 March 2001, all American stomachs were thinking of tacos from Taco Bell. The Mexican-style restaurant had placed a 144-square-metre target in the South Pacific Ocean, near where the shuttle was expected to land, and offered every American a free taco if 'Mir rings our bell'.

Although Mir was expected to land in the ocean somewhere in an area 200km wide and 6000km long between New Zealand and Chile, Taco Bell purchased an insurance policy to cover the anticipated cost should it hit the target.

Advertiser **Taco Bell Corp**
USA 2001

AMPLIFICATION EFFECT
Through television coverage alone, the stunt reached more than 120 million people.

'We've even heard about consumers chanting T-A-C-O, T-A-C-O as Mir descended.'

Laurie Schalow, public relations, Taco Bell Corp.

226

In three football games in a row, every time Brazilian star player Mário Jardel scored a goal for his Portuguese team, he revealed his under T-shirt that read: 'I wonder why?'. The media speculated about the cryptic message, surmising that it could be a personal message to his trainer, who had not called him to play on the national team, or a political reference as it happened during the elections.

The speculation ended during a decisive match between the country's two biggest rival teams. Once again Jardel scored and showed his under T-shirt, this time reading: 'Is it the Guaraná?'. Guaraná Antártica, Brazil's national soft drink, had been launched in Portugal as the magic potion that unleashed the Brazilian spirit. The television commercial had revolved around a young girl lifting her shirt after striking a goal during a football match on the beach.

Client **AMBEV**
Agency **BBDO Portugal**
Portugal 2002

AMPLIFICATION EFFECT
During the campaign, the Jardel stunt made front-page news at some point in every newspaper. Even television stations took interest in the campaign.

Later, the image of Jardel revealing the Guaraná message was turned into a print advertising campaign.

227

To launch the Fiat Panda in the UK, the car's name was used as the basis for the whole campaign: 'A new breed of Panda'. Part of the campaign involved dressing the Cherhill Wiltshire White Horse in black vinyl to extend the visual theme.

Print, posters and direct mails used the strengths of different animals to demonstrate the new car's attributes.

Client **Fiat**
Agency **ARC**
UK 2004

A Panda that goes 50 mpg

A new breed of Panda **FIAT**

228

Getting a work of art for 10p prompted hundreds of people to queue at Tate Britain in London, as work by young British artist Gavin Turk was printed on the Xerox DocuColor 2240. Turk signed the prints to authenticate the offering.

Client **Xerox**
Agency **Harrison Troughton Wunderman**
UK 2002

'By tying the event into the brand and product strategies, it is not by chance that we sold more products in the UK than the whole of the US in quarter 4 2002.'

Richard Wergan, head of communications for Xerox Europe

AMPLIFICATION EFFECT
To attract members of the public and journalists to the event, a press ad and poster were created. Postcards were mailed to journalists and handed out at art colleges and in trendy bars. The event received over £50,000 of coverage.

The sales force at Xerox used the event as an opportunity to contact 200 of their top customers to invite them to the launch.

Another Young British Artist sells a piece of their work for a ridiculous amount of money.

How much could you pay for a signed piece of work by a famous Young British Artist. £5,000, £10,000 or a whole lot more?

But, how much *should* you pay? And *who* sets the price anyway?

Well, on Wednesday 18th September, Gavin Turk will be turning the 'value of art' on its head. Using affordable digital technology – the new

Xerox DocuColor 2240 – he'll be creating perfect colour copies of his work, signing them and then selling them for the price it costs to print them. Just 10p!

This will be happening in the Clore Foyer, at Tate Britain, for 45 minutes only from 12:30pm.

So come along and buy one. Who knows how much your 10p print will be worth in the future?

There's a new way to look at things.

THE DOCUMENT COMPANY
XEROX.

229

For the launch of their Asian edition, *The Financial Times* 'wrapped' Hong Kong's tallest building at that time. This feat earned them a place in *The Guinness Book of Records* for the world's largest outdoor announcement.

Client **The Financial Times**
Agency **Mediaedge:CIA**
China 2003

AMPLIFICATION EFFECT
The simple yet impactful image of the tower travelled around the world in no time.

230

To promote *FHM*'s '100 Sexiest Women' poll, the image of Gail Porter was projected onto the Houses of Parliament in London. What better place to advertise voting for sexy women than the UK's most famous voting institution?

Client **FHM**
Agency **Cunning**
UK 1999

AMPLIFICATION EFFECT
With coverage in every tabloid and broadsheet together with numerous broadcasts, the projection is probably one of the most famous PR stunts of all time, winning Radio 4's Stunt of the 20th Century.

Practical advice

Building campaigns
Building brands with bricks
Dropping the big one
Elite campaigns
Micro campaigns
Curtain campaigns
Mystery campaigns

Twenty pointers to start you thinking

Building campaigns

There was a time when unconventional advertising techniques were reserved only for the small and local brands, the ones that operated within a small geographic area, that were in search of a very specific target group or that had limited budgets. These brands or companies logically avoid mass media since it would result in wasted money and would not allow them to reach their target group directly. Big brands rarely used or integrated unconventional media in their overall campaign picture, and if they did, it was usually an isolated instance.

Since the mid 1990s, and even more so in the beginning of the new millennium, non-traditional techniques have been used increasingly alongside or instead of traditional media channels as a way to counter the latter's decreasing efficiency. There is growing awareness that alternative channels need to be carefully integrated within the broader communication architecture and need to be in line with the overall message of the brand. This chapter explores how this smooth integration can be realized.

Building brands with bricks

Brands are not built like puzzles. Comparing a brand with a puzzle suggests that there is only one correct combination of its multiple pieces. It suggests that the overall campaign architecture has been perfectly designed beforehand, and all the 'players' have to do is reconstruct it. It is quite the contrary. All a brand does and can do is send out different pieces, whether it is a press release, an ad on television, a branded event, a sampling action or an online game. It is down to the audience to create their own specific combination, keeping and remembering what they like and ignoring what they do not like. A comparison with LEGO bricks, made by Mediaedge:CIA[28], is much more apt since it describes a two-way, dynamic process. LEGO bricks can be combined in endless ways and it is the person building with the bricks who decides what the final construction will look like.

In other words, branding is a two-way dynamic process. **Brands are multilayered, multifaceted constructions that come to life in the minds of consumers.** Brands are not finished constructions that can be handed to consumers, but they can spread the bricks in the hope that consumers will pick them up and use them.

Dropping the big one

This top-down versus bottom-up vision of brands is reflected in the way brands use media channels. Brands that communicate from the top down rely more heavily on mass media; those that believe in building a brand from the bottom up turn more to alternative channels and media.

Campaigns that rely heavily or solely on mass media reflect the belief that the story of a brand is universal and monolithic and needs to be transmitted at a given moment to the entire population. This results in 'big-bang' (and big-budget) campaigning, addressing as many people as possible in as little time as possible. In war terminology, it is dropping 'the big one'. It is not subtle, nor is it supposed to be. Built on the logic that as many people as possible should see, hear or come into contact with the same message, it is the sort of communication campaign from which no escape is possible. However, it is exactly this kind of behaviour that convinces consumers of a brand's domineering and bulldozing tactics.

The idea that a brand can direct the whole picture in a single communication is an illusion. Consider a relationship between two people: we do not win people over through one defining speech or moment, but through a multitude of everyday actions and words. **Guerrilla warfare is much the same: the final victory is the result of a series of separate events and strikes, each in response to a specific situation or challenge.**

As a consequence, how media channels and tactics are used must be reviewed. If it is not necessarily best to communicate to everybody at the same time, the appeal of mass media as a key brand-building instrument diminishes. Instead, it opens up the possibilities for more targeted and unconventional campaign architectures.

When building a communication campaign, four main components can be played with: the target group, the message, the timing and the communication channels. Any story can be broken up into separate stories that address separate groups of people at separate moments in time through separate channels. This fragmented, brick-building view of campaigning leads to interesting new campaign constructions. Four specific constructions stand out: elite campaigns that privilege specific groups of people; micro campaigns that relay different stories to different groups of people; curtain campaigns that tell the story little by little; and mystery campaigns that spread fragmented, unfinished messages.

Elite campaigns

Traditional advertising campaigns speak to everybody, but to nobody in particular. They address mass audiences but do not acknowledge the special status, needs or habits of specific groups of people. Elite campaigns, on the other hand, give some people within a target group a more privileged treatment. **They are designed to make a group of people feel special, to make them feel as if a brand is truly speaking to them – and nobody else.** While traditional advertising campaigns are huge concerts, elite campaigns are invitation-only, backstage performances for a select group of people. There are two ways to accomplish this: by giving one group of people information *before* others or by giving them *more* information than others. These people might be trendsetters, connectors or innovators, people who have the power to spread the word quickly or who have an influence on others. They might also be loyal customers, who a brand wishes to reward. Giving these people special, exclusive attention is the best way to create and enhance brand ambassadorship. For example, if a company is about to reveal a new logo or communication campaign, it might be beneficial to inform its most loyal customers first. Before the launch of a new game or movie, an elite campaign can target bloggers, who are experts in these domains, by sending them special versions, extras or information. By doing this, a brand acknowledges their status within the community and can, therefore, positively influence their opinion. This strategy was used for *Halo 2*, the second version of a hugely popular video game that runs on Microsoft's Xbox. Eighteen months before the game hit the shops, it was handed out to an 'inner circle' of committed players to create a buzz of excitement. When it was finally launched, it raked in over $100 million in sales on its first day.[29]

Mini Cooper adopted an elite campaign for its launch in the UK. While a typical car launch involves a blockbuster television ad supported by double-page spreads in the Sunday supplements and

perhaps a large chunk of money spent on outdoor advertising, Mini chose to target innovators 6 months before the launch.[30] Mini Open Air Theatre (see campaign 171, p. 158) was performed in the centre of London and created the necessary buzz around the car. That is what elite campaigns are about: giving a limited number of people special treatment, with the clear intention of spreading buzz to a larger group of people. 'Marketers are learning to turn their brands into carefully guarded secrets that are revealed to a knowing few in each community,' according to an article on Buzz Marketing. These few people 'in turn tell a few more, who tell a few more, and so on.' Instead of blitzing the airways with 30-second television commercials for its new Focus subcompact, Ford Motor Company recruited a handful of trendsetters in a few markets and gave them each a Focus to drive for six months. They simply needed to be seen with the car and hand out Focus-themed trinkets to anyone who expressed interest in it.[31]

So whatever the product, brand or target audience, it is essential to work out who the elite is, which set of people is best suited to function as ambassadors for the brand or simply deserves special treatment. Find out who they are, their characteristics, where they live or hang out, and then start a campaign that makes these people feel as if they truly are elite. **Successful elite campaigns accomplish what most communication campaigns can only hope to do: to make people feel as if a brand is speaking directly to them.**

Micro campaigns

While elite campaigns privilege one specific group of people, micro campaigns address a series of different target groups, each in a different way. The idea is that a brand has various meanings for different people, dependent on their age, social status, gender, sexual preference, profession, and so on. Pleasure, refreshment and excitement mean different things for different groups of people. Micro campaigns acknowledge that and therefore have a much greater chance of reaching people in the most effective and relevant way. It is something that conventional mass-media advertising is incapable of doing. Seth Godin compares traditional advertising with hurricanes, 'whipping through a marketplace horizontally, touching everyone in the same way, regardless of who they are and what they want'. He draws the conclusion that 'it is useless to advertise to anyone'[32]. Communication should be less like a shot gun and more like a rifle shot, aiming precisely at the right people with the right message and the right medium.[33] Larry Light, McDonald's chief marketing officer, refers to this approach as 'brand journalism', saying that 'any single ad, commercial or promotion ... is not representative of the brand message. We don't need one big execution of a big idea. We need one big idea that can be used in a multidimensional, multilayered and multifaceted way.'[34]

This idea also became apparent to Procter & Gamble. When research showed that girls wanted to know more about Tampax, the company shifted a chunk of advertising from television to print and created a website called Beinggirl.com. 'It's hard to convey a lot of information and stuff that's kind of personal in a 30-second TV ad,' says Ted Woehrle, vice-president for North American marketing[35]. Micro campaigns rest on the belief that there is not one particular way to communicate a story to an audience, but there are as many ways as there are types of consumers. **Brands need to act like chameleons, adapting to the specific environment of their different groups of customers.** Instead of producing the one print ad or commercial that is plastered everywhere, a campaign can be the sum of endless executions. This creates many opportunities for alternative media techniques that were previously deemed too niche or too targeted. Instead of selling washing powder to the whole nation on prime-time television, you could communicate the powder to a number of relevant target groups: to business people through corporate events, to teenage girls through installations in trendy shopping outlets, to housewives through house parties, and so on. The overall effect is that people feel as if the brand has addressed them in a more personal way and has made the effort to connect with their specific situation and lifestyle.

This level of personalization clearly demands more effort and is a more labour-intensive assignment than mass-approach advertising. For a salesman, it is a much easier and less demanding task to tell the same story again and again to every one of his customers, rather than having to adapt that story to each customer profile. Yet a successful salesman stresses different elements of his product to suit the person

he is selling to. Alan Schulman introduced the term 'scenarios' in this respect. He claims that the same idea can be transformed into endless variations by using different scenarios, since 'different scenarios are required to be relevant to different targets'[36].

There is no limit to how specific and targeted micro campaigns can be. The ultimate goal is to have a different story for every individual, so that brand communication becomes a strictly personal conversation.

Curtain campaigns

I previously compared advertising with a game of hide and seek between brands and consumers. This is reflected by this category and the following one: curtain and mystery campaigns. Curtain campaigns do not lay all their cards on the table from the first moment since it would spoil the game, but they deliberately spread pieces of information, little by little revealing the bigger story, like a curtain slowly exposing a stage. Examples are Mini Cooper's robot story (see campaign 145, p. 136) and Sega's Beta-7 story (see campaign 143, p. 134). Both spread specific pieces of a larger story, feeding people with partial information and not revealing the complete story until the very last moment. **Curtain campaigns consciously choose to reveal their story piecemeal to keep their audience hungry for more and to make them interact with the story while it is being built.**

In film marketing, the teaser-trailer process is a typical example of a curtain campaign. This two-step process is a classic yet effective way to build up tension gradually before the launch of a movie. Teasers grab our attention and can be mysterious and vague; trailers fill in the blanks and give the bigger picture. For the teaser-trailer split to generate enough tension, it needs to be carefully set up and paid off, to use movie-making vocabulary. First, the teaser needs to arouse enough curiosity to make people long for what follows. Second, the trailer needs to fulfil the expectations raised by the teaser. In other words, teasers and trailers need to be strongly linked.

This two-step process can also be applied to brand communication. Consider two examples featured in this book that have successfully spread their message this way. The Portuguese launch of the Brazilian soft drink Guaraná (see campaign 226, p. 201) started with a mysterious question on the T-shirt of one of Brazil's star football players, which he revealed live during matches. It was unclear to the audience and the press who was behind the question and what the answer was. It therefore created the necessary buzz in the press. During one of the most important matches of the season, the answer was revealed, again on his T-shirt. The link between the set-up and the pay-off was logical and clear and resulted in much awareness and buzz around the new soft drink. *nzgirl*, an online magazine for young girls, created much the same hype when it had an airplane fly over a concert crowd carrying the message 'Scott Kelly has got a small dick' (see campaign 147, p. 137). Since there was no signature, it remained unclear who either Scott Kelly or the creator of the message was. Later, a second aeroplane revealed that *nzgirl* was responsible. The action generated much word of mouth thanks to the two steps in which the information was sent out. If both messages had been communicated simultaneously, the impact would have been far smaller.

Communication campaigns are most often driven by a fast build-up of awareness, conveying as much information as possible at the same time, leaving no time for several phases. Sometimes, however, it can prove worthwhile to pause for breath and think a few steps ahead. *The Blair Witch Project* is the most famous example in marketing history of a curtain campaign and began its first subtle marketing efforts two years before the launch of the movie. It was precisely the calculated and slow build-up that made it one of the most successful and talked about curtain campaigns in recent history.

Mystery campaigns
While curtain campaigns reveal some kind of finished story in the end and have a logical build-up over time, mystery campaigns do not. Mystery campaigns are a string of separate, seemingly unrelated components, with no overtly logical build-up or storyline. Why should all communication be a perfectly neat and finished story with a clear build-up, a beginning and an end? That is not how it always

works in real life. **Understanding that today's consumers are smarter and ever more experienced at decoding advertising campaigns, advertising has the right, or even the duty, to be more enigmatic, mysterious and subtle.** By cultivating mystique, brands leave it up to their audience to compose the picture and tie up the loose ends. Instead of telling the brand story in a very overt and complete way, campaigns can also interest people by communicating ideas without clear resolution. When online music provider Napster relaunched its services, it conducted a campaign that was all tease and no resolution. They slapped kitty head (the company's logo) stickers over other ads throughout the city and set up a microsite. According to Paul Venables, creative director at Venables Bell & Partners, 'the idea is to tease, period. Not as part of the bigger campaign, not as a glimpse of what's to come. That, we feel, would be too perfect a communication, therefore too corporate.' It is precisely this raw, unfinished nature that appeals to today's savvy audience. When Wrangler jeans put ice blocks on cars in German cities (see campaign 107, p. 104), it was not immediately clear why and nobody bothered to explain it. But that was also the charm of the action. According to Secret Lives, a study conducted by the Singapore-based agency Red Card, this kind of 'inadvertent brand contact is perhaps the only truly effective brand communications tool. Accidental, incidental, and apparently unpredictable, it is built on seemingly unconnected chance encounters, interwoven and interconnected like brand hyperlinks, revealing the brand slowly, intelligently, flirtatiously, making the consumer do the work, not pouring it out in one execution.'[37]

Twenty pointers to start you thinking

With so many new methods at our disposal, the search for remarkable unconventional communication solutions and ideas has become wild and chaotic. For some, the multitude of opportunities can have a paralyzing effect, so here are 20 pointers to help you to begin exploring the vast landscape of possibilities.

1. Can you do what your brand promises?

Many brand promises have a hollow, advertising-like ring to them; 'brand overpromise' is often closer to the truth. Brands send the savvy consumer running for the hills, because such consumers dislike and, where possible, avoid companies that make claims that sound false.[38] Therefore, it is essential to consider the ways in which you can make a brand promise come to life. Instead of simply claiming such things as 'the battery lasts longer', 'the service is better', 'the car outstrips all others', 'the drink is more refreshing', back up these statements with tangible actions. Do not say you are moving mountains, just move them.

How others did it
87 Toyota pp 88–89 • 88 Bosch p. 89 • 189 Colgate Palmolive p. 171 • 204 Tango p. 183 • 214 DaimlerChrysler p. 193 • 219 & 220 Adidas pp 196–97

2. Can you demonstrate or visualize the brand or product three-dimensionally?

Imagine that all two-dimensional media (print, television, cinema) had ceased to exist. How would you convey your brand in a three-dimensional way?

How others did it
64 Virgin Atlantic p. 71 • 65 Hapag-Lloyd Express p. 73 • 66 Olympus p. 74 • 72 Volkswagen p. 79 • 78 Virgin Atlantic p. 83 • 80 Hewlett-Packard p. 85 • 84 Adopt-A-Minefield p. 87 • 90 KFM Radio p. 91 • 101 & 102 Mini p. 99 • 105 Kraft Foods pp 102–03 • 118 Nike p. 114 • 149 Channel 9 p. 139 • 150 Paton Fertilizers p. 140 • 154 Unilever p. 144

3. Can you create sensory experiences around your product or brand?

Describe what the product delivers in terms of taste, smell, sound, vision or touch. Find ways to make one or more of the five senses come to life.

How others did it
176 BMW p. 164 • 186 Affinity Petcare p. 170 • 187 DaimlerChrysler p. 171 • 188 Bauducco & CIA p. 171 • 189 Colgate Palmolive p. 171 • 190 Canderel p. 172 • 191 Philips p. 173

4. Be creative with the appearance – form, shape, colour, size, name, logo – of your product or brand.

List everything that strongly resembles or relates to the external characteristics of your product. For a battery, for example, note things that are long and cylinder-shaped. If the brand icon contains a specific figure or symbol, write down other places where it can be found. Make surprising and unexpected connections. If your product or brand is less tangible, find visual metaphors and associations. For example, Amnesty International used imagery of fences, prison bars and torture weapons. Look for ways to incorporate them into your message.

How others did it
17 Forte 1000 condoms/phallic symbols p. 34 • **18** World Revival Prayer Fellowship/cross shapes p. 34 • **22 & 23** Amnesty International/gates and prison bars pp 36–37 • **24** British Airways' legroom/barriers p. 38 • **25** Nintendo Game Cube/sugar cubes p. 38 • **85 & 86** Blood Transfusion Services & Red Cross Singapore/red ink p. 87 • **92–95** Absolut/iconic bottle shape pp 94–95 • **106** Maryland Cookies/UFO p. 102 • **163** Dunlop/tyre pattern p. 151

5. When you have an idea for a traditional piece of advertising – such as a print ad or a television commercial – develop that idea one stage further and take it along the non-conventional route.

Truly great ideas often work across a wide array of disciplines, both traditional and non-traditional. A great idea for a print ad or a television commercial might just as easily be translated beyond the realm of traditional advertising into an effective event or online game.

How others did it
92–95 Absolut pp 94–95 • **169** sperm men p. 156 • **202** Reebok p. 182 • **204** Tango p. 183

6. Use traditional media channels in ways they have not been used before.

Traditional media channels offer plenty of opportunities to be creative. Take magazines: all kinds of variables can be played with, including the sort of paper, the printing technique, the placement within the magazine and the size of the page. Television, newspapers, cinema, radio and outdoor media always offer new creative and unexplored opportunities.

How others did it
12 SBAB p. 31 • **95** Absolut p. 95 • **98** IKEA p. 97 • **122** Mercedes-Benz p. 116 • **134** Senna Import p. 125 • **156** Mini p. 145 • **158** Delta Motor Corporation p. 146 • **175** *The Economist* p. 163 • **176** BMW p. 164 • **179** ABC Literacy p. 166 • **182** Diageo p. 167 • **185** VAG Group p. 169 • **191** Senseo p. 173 • **196** SBAB p. 177 • **199** McDonald's p. 180 • **219** Adidas p. 196

7. Create the ideal setting in which your product or brand is experienced.

Quite often, there is a wide gap between the way a brand is portrayed in advertising and how it translates into real life. To close the gap between advertising fiction and consumer reality, create the ideal but realistic circumstances in which your product or brand should be experienced. If your brand is about cosiness and conviviality, create an atmosphere that perfectly mimics these qualities. Try to simulate or re-create the best possible brand or product encounter that can be played out in everyday life.

How others did it
99 Interbrew p. 98 • 165 Gafisa p. 153 • 171 Mini Cooper pp 158–59 • 184 Procter & Gamble p. 168 • 189 Colgate Palmolive p. 171 • 190 Canderel p. 172 • 198 Meow Mix p. 179 • 200 Nike p. 180 • 207 Norwich Union p. 185 • 208 Hewlett-Packard p. 187

8. Where would be the most surprising place for your product or brand to appear?

Search out places where people would not expect to encounter your product or brand, but would be pleasantly surprised to do so.

How others did it
10 Pidilite Industries p. 30 • 104 Clorox p. 100 • 96 IKEA p. 96 • 98 IKEA p. 97 • 103 The Protestant Church pp 100–01 • 109 DaimlerChrysler p. 105 • 183 Flex Mattresses p. 168

9. Find things – objects, places, television programmes, films – that are associated with your product or brand. Find ways to make connections.

If your product is cigarettes, associated objects would include ashtrays, lighters, matches, special cigarette cases; associated places would be smoking areas in companies, restaurants or public spaces and the sidewalks around big companies where people stand and smoke; associated content would include all television programmes or films in which characters smoke. Try using these objects and places, or try mixing them into your communication.

How others did it
13 Duracell p. 31 • 26 K2r p. 39 • 44 Evian pp 52–53 • 58 Illy p. 67 • 61 *The Guardian* p. 69 • 62 Unicef p. 70 • 63 Sydney Dogs Home p. 70 • 71 Singapore Cancer Society p. 78 • 79 Nike p. 84 • 83 Nike p. 86 • 89 PlayStation pp 90–91

10. Play tricks on your audience.

Cunning visual or auditory illusions are not only a welcome source of amusement, they also have the ability to grab the attention of your audience. Find ways to play with the perception of your audience.

How others did it

11. Use everything that you own as a communication medium.

Note in detail all the spaces you own, from the product's packaging to company letters, from staff clothing to company vehicles. Find creative ways of using these spaces or integrating them into your overall campaign.

How others did it

12. Investigate ways to team up with like-minded brands or products.

List all brands – preferably outside your sector – that offer the experience or proposition with which you want to be associated. If you want your brand to credibly communicate good-old-fashioned family values, consider all the brands that cover this terrain. If you want to focus your brand on luxury, list the brands and products that already incorporate this. Then, find ways to make connections with these brands.

How others did it

13. Invent a compelling story starring your brand or product.

Unleash the storyteller from within. Do not think of your brand or product as a 30-second commercial or a single image. Instead, think of it as a super story, a lengthy drama or a screenplay for a feature film. Devise a story with a plot that stars your brand or product. Ensure that the story is credible, compelling and entertaining.

How others did it

14. Think outrageously. Think bigger than life. Think megalomaniac.

Do not be too low-key in your thinking, after all you want to capture people's attention. Forget for a moment that you may not be the worldwide leader in your category. If your product is a running shoe, have people run from one end of the planet to the other.

How others did it
44 Evian pp 52–53 • 68 J-Wave p. 76 • 105 Kraft Foods pp 102–03 • 106 Maryland Cookies p. 102 • 211 Virgin Cola p. 191 • 216 Nintendo p. 194 • 219 & 220 Adidas pp 196–97 • 225 Taco Bell p. 201

15. Find ways to make your brand or product newsworthy.

Any product or brand has the potential to be newsworthy, all it takes is a spark of creativity. Search for ways to connect your brand or product to something that is already in the news.

How others did it
198 Meow Mix p. 179 • 211 Virgin Cola p. 191 • 216 Nintendo p. 194 • 219 & 220 Adidas pp 196–97 • 221 Foundation for Physically Disabled Persons p. 198 • 222 UIP p. 199 • 223 Virgin Records p. 200 • 224 Virgin Express p. 200 • 225 Taco Bell p. 201 • 226 AMBEV p. 201 • 227 Fiat p. 202 • 228 Xerox p. 203 • 229 *The Financial Times* p. 204 • 230 *FHM* p. 205

16. Who would you choose to sell your brand or product? Would it be a single person or a clearly defined group?

Who are the best imaginable salesmen or ambassadors for your brand or product? They might be attractive young men and women, wise old men, computer geeks or housewives. Describe them in as much detail as possible and then research ways to involve them or give them a special treatment.

How others did it
6 Specsavers p. 27 • 58 Illy p. 67 • 160 Carabineros de Chile p. 149 • 164 UIP p. 152 • 200 Nike p. 180 • 208 Hewlett-Packard p. 187 • 218 SBAB p. 196 • 221 Foundation for Physically Disabled Persons p. 198 • 222 UIP p. 199 • 223 Virgin Records p. 200 • 226 AMBEV p. 201 • 228 Xerox p. 203

17. Be present where your audience is.

The only way to really get to know somebody is by walking in his or her shoes. To understand where and how your consumers live, follow them for a certain period of time, much like behavioural scientists would do. Be present in all the public and private places – shops, outlets, buildings, cities, areas, special venues – where your target group congregates on a regular basis.

How others did it

30 & 31 Red Cross Croatia and Salvation Army Singapore/clothing shops pp 42–43 • **32** Playground outdoor equipment specialist/people's bikes p. 43 • **33** Canal+/football stadia p. 44 • **34** Nike/football pitches p. 45 • **38** Nike/marathons pp 48–49 • **61** *The Guardian*/golf courses p. 69 • **131** Nike/parks p. 123

18. Involve the target group in your story.

Make your target group feel as if they are part of the brand. This can range from contests to large-scale events, from interactive games to opinion polls, just as long as you actively include them instead of passively spreading your message.

How others did it

96 IKEA p. 96 • **185** VAG Group p. 169 • **192** Burger King p. 175 • **193** Mobilkom Austria p. 176 • **194** Swedoor p. 176 • **196** SBAB p. 177 • **197** Campbell p. 178 • **198** Meow Mix p. 179 • **199** McDonald's p. 180 • **200** Nike p. 180 • **202** Reebok p. 182 • **204** Tango p. 183 • **206** PlayStation p. 184 • **207** Norwich Union p. 185 • **222** UIP p. 199

19. Hand over power to the consumers. Consider ways to put them in complete control.

Allow the consumers to be the true rulers of your brand. All you need to do is create the environment within which they can reign and then let go.

How others did it

208 Hewlett-Packard p. 187 • **210** Coca-Cola p. 189

20. What can you do for your customers to make their day?

Instead of overloading consumers with information or witty campaigns, why not help them for real? Be altruistic for a change; think about what they would like. Make their day. Chances are that they will thank and remember you for it.

How others did it

42 Molson USA p. 51 • **44** Evian p. 53 • **96** IKEA p. 96 • **137** T-Mobile p. 128 • **183** Flex Mattresses p. 168 • **184** Procter & Gamble p. 168 • **190** Canderel p. 172 • **201** Smirnoff p. 181 • **208** Hewlett-Packard p. 187

Notes

1 Jeff Hicks in PICCALO G. 'The pitch that you won't see coming.' *Chicago Tribune*, 22 August 2004.

2 HALL E. and MADDEN N. 'Ikea's Global Reach Bows to Local Culture.' *AdAge*, 12 April 2004.

3 http://www.trendwatching.com/trends/TRYVERTISING.htm

4 AUSTIN M. and AITCHINSON J. *Is Anybody Out There? The New Blueprint for Marketing Communications in the 21st Century*. John Wiley & Sons, 2003, p. 116.

5 ATKINSON C. 'Broadcast TV Networks Rattled by DVR Inroads.' *AdAge*, 11 April 2005.

6 AUSTIN M. and AITCHINSON J. *Is Anybody Out There? The New Blueprint for Marketing Communications in the 21st Century*. John Wiley & Sons, 2003, p. 43.

7 ALDHOUS C. in JAFFE J. *Life After the 30-second Spot. Energize Your Brand with a Bold Mix of Alternatives to Traditional Advertising*. John Wiley & Sons, 2005, p. 183.

8 URBANO, 'Fighting in the Streets: a Manual of Urban Guerrilla Warfare', p. 9.

9 SACHARIN K. *Attention! How to interrupt, yell, whisper, and touch consumers...* (Adweek book series) John Wiley & Sons, 2000, p. 96.

10 AUSTIN M. and AITCHINSON J. *Is Anybody Out There? The New Blueprint for Marketing Communications in the 21st Century*. John Wiley & Sons, 2003, p. 157.

11 http://knowledge.wharton.upenn.edu/article/1105.cfm. 'What's the Buzz about Buzz Marketing?', 12 January 2005.

12 WALKER R. 'The Hidden (in Plain Sight) Persuaders.' *The New York Times Magazine*, 5 December 2004, p. 69.

13 KAYE K. 'Sales Pitch Society, how advertisers get us to do their dirty work.' *The Lowbrow Lowdown*, 2001. http://www.salespitchsociety.com

14 GILMORE JAMES H. and PINE B. JOSEPH. *The Experience Economy, Work Is Theater & Every Business a Stage*. HBS Press, 1999, pp 132–33.

15 Ibid, p. 59.

16 Ibid, p. 59.

17 LINDSTROM M. *Brand Sense: Build Powerful Brands through Touch, Taste, Smell, Sight, and Sound*. Free Press, 2005.

18 GILMORE JAMES H. and PINE B. JOSEPH. *The Experience Economy, Work Is Theater & Every Business a Stage*. HBS Press, 1999, p. 59.

19 Ibid, p. 59.

20 http://www.trendwatching.com

21 MACDONALD G. 'What's In It For Me?' *Contagious Magazine*, October 2004, p. 39.

22 ALDHOUS C. in JAFFE J. *Life After the 30-second Spot. Energize Your Brand with a Bold Mix of Alternatives to Traditional Advertising*. John Wiley & Sons, 2005, p. 184.

23 BORKOWSKI M. *Improperganda. The Art of the Publicity Stunt*. Vision on Publishing, 2000, p. 7.

24 ROSEN E. *The Anatomy of Buzz, How to Create Word-of-mouth Marketing*. Currency, 2000.

25 SANGHERA S. 'Can Matthew Freud be serious?' *The Financial Times*, 2 December 2001.

26 ZYMAN S. *The End of Advertising As We Know It*. John Wiley & Sons, 2002, p. 179.

27 BOND J. and KIRSHENBAUM R. *Under the Radar: Talking to Today's Cynical Consumer*. (Adweek Book series) John Wiley & Sons, 1997, p. 54.

28 MEDIAEDGE:CIA 'Connecting with the new consumer. The case for a new approach to brand communication', 2002.

29 MARKILLIE P. 'Target Practice. Advertising used to be straightforward, now it has to be many different things to different people.' *The Economist*, 2 April 2005.

30 SAUNDERS J. *Communications Challenge, A Practical Guide to Media Neutral Planning*. The Account Planning Group, 2004, pp 92–93.

31 GREEN J. and KHERMOUCH G. 'Buzz Marketing, Suddenly this Stealth Strategy is Hot – but it's still Fraught with Risk.' *BusinessWeek*, 30 July 2001.

32 GODIN S. *Purple Cow. Transform Your Business by Being Remarkable*. Prototype, 2003, p. 35.

33 MARKILLIE P. 'Target Practice. Advertising used to be straightforward, now it has to be many different things to different people.' *The Economist*, 2 April 2005.

34 Larry Light, McDonald's Corp's chief marketing officer, during a conference at the Cannes International Advertising Festival 2004.

35 BYRNES N., BERNER R., ZELLNER W., SYMONDS, W. 'Branding: Five New Lessons.' *BusinessWeek*, 14 February 2005.

36 SCHULMAN A. 'The New Creative Imperative.' *Brand New World*, 18 August 2004.

37 AUSTIN M. and AITCHINSON J. *Is Anybody Out There? The New Blueprint for Marketing Communications in the 21st Century*. John Wiley & Sons, 2003, p. 44.

38 BLOOM J. 'Wrestling Marketers Down to Naked Reality.' *AdAge*, 21 March 2005.

Glossary

Advergaming

Advergaming uses games, particularly computer games, to advertise or promote a product, organization or viewpoint. The brand, product or company cleverly packages and translates its message into an interactive gaming experience.

Ambient advertising

Referring to intrusive ads in public places, ambient advertising takes as a premise that anything can be used as a vehicle for advertising. Ambient ads appear on store floors, on beer mats, in bar toilets, at gas pumps, on elevator walls, on park benches, on telephones, on fruit and even imprinted on the sand at beaches.

Ambush marketing

Ambush marketing occurs when one brand pays to become an official sponsor of an event and another competing brand attempts to cleverly connect itself with the event, without paying the sponsorship fee. Ambush marketing is as undeniably effective as it is damaging, attracting consumers at the expense of competitors, all the while undermining an event's integrity and its ability to attract future sponsors.

Branded content or branded entertainment

The integration of brands into the content of various media (such as television and radio), as well as the creation of original content built around brands. Branded content includes the creation of short films, feature films, television programmes, documentaries, and so on, in which the brand plays a clearly identifiable role. Also known as content integration.

Buzz marketing

When people are prompted in some way to share information about products or promotions with friends it is known as buzz marketing. A marketer successfully creates a buzz when interactions are so intense that the information moves in a matrix pattern, rather than a linear one, and everyone is talking about the brand. There is a clear distinction between buzz marketing and stealth or undercover marketing: buzz marketing listens to consumers and gives them a voice, stealth or undercover marketing tricks people. Also known as word of mouth, wildfire, viral marketing.

Content integration

See branded content or branded entertainment

Experiential marketing

Actual consumer interactions with products for the purpose of driving product sales. It is the difference between telling people about features or benefits within the confines of a 30-second TV spot and letting them experience these things and have their own moment of revelation.

Grassroots marketing

See guerrilla advertising

Guerrilla advertising or marketing

The term 'guerrilla' is the Spanish for 'little war'. Guerrilla marketing is an unconventional way of performing marketing activities on a limited budget. Also known as grassroots marketing.

Product placement

Product placement integrates an advertiser's product into non-commercial content, such as television programmes, feature films, radio programmes or news articles. Product placement helps advertisers to reach consumers in a seemingly indirect fashion. It is almost always arranged in exchange for financial compensation.

Referral marketing

Referral marketing is closely related to viral marketing and concerns marketing efforts that encourage the referral of a brand, product or business between people. For example, some marketers have made clever use of the blogging community — such as giving them special samples — so that bloggers would 'refer' people to their products or services.

Stealth marketing

See undercover marketing

Street marketing

A term that covers a variety of marketing activities carried out in the public domain, including hand-to-hand distribution, retail drops, wild postings of posters and stickers, product samples, giveaways, and much more.

Undercover marketing

Undercover marketing is a technique in which the consumers do not realize they are being targeted. For example, a marketing company might pay a consumer or socially adept person to use a certain product visibly and convincingly in locations where target consumers congregate. While there, the consumer talks up the product to the people he or she befriends and may even hand out samples if feasible. The actor is often able to convince consumers about the product without those consumers even noticing it. The actor must look and sound like a peer of the target audience and must seem to have no ulterior motive for endorsing the product. Also known as stealth marketing or (by its detractors) roach baiting.

Viral marketing

Marketing techniques that try to exploit existing social networks to create an exponential increase in brand awareness, much like the spread of a virus. For instance, entertaining films or stories can spread globally via the Internet in a matter of days or hours. Also known as buzz marketing, wildfire, word of mouth.

Wildfire

See buzz marketing
Also known as viral marketing and word of mouth.

Word of mouth marketing

See buzz marketing
Also known as viral marketing, wildfire.

Bibliography

Books

AUSTIN M. and AITCHINSON J. *Is Anybody Out There? The New Blueprint for Marketing Communications in the 21st Century*. John Wiley & Sons, 2003.

BOND J. and KIRSHENBAUM R. *Under the Radar: Talking to Today's Cynical Consumer*. (Adweek Book series) John Wiley & Sons, 1997.

BORKOWSKI M. *Improperganda. The Art of the Publicity Stunt*. Vision on Publishing, 2000.

CAPPO J. *The Future of Advertising. New Media, New Clients, New Consumers in the Post-Television Age*. AdvertisingAge, 2003.

GILMORE JAMES H. and PINE B. JOSEPH *The Experience Economy, Work Is Theater & Every Business a Stage*. HBS Press, 1999.

GLADWELL M. *The Tipping Point*. Abacus, 2002.

GODIN S. *Purple Cow. Transform Your Business by Being Remarkable*. Prototype, 2003.

GODIN S. *Unleashing the Ideavirus*. Do You Zoom, Inc., 2000.

GOLDSMITH R. *Viral Marketing, Get your audience to do your marketing for you*. Pearson Education, 2002.

HOROWITZ S. *Grassroots Marketing, Getting Noticed in a Noisy World*. Chelsea Green Publishing Company, 2000.

JAFFE J. *Life After the 30-second Spot. Energize Your Brand with a Bold Mix of Alternatives to Traditional Advertising*. John Wiley & Sons, 2005.

KAPLAN THALER L., KOVAL R. and MARSHALL D. *Bang! Getting Your Message Heard in a Noisy World*. Currency, 2003.

LEVINSON JAY CONRAD *Guerrilla Marketing. Secrets for Making Big Profits From Your Small Business*. Houghton Mifflin Company, 1998.

LINDSTROM M. *Brand Sense: Build Powerful Brands through Touch, Taste, Smell, Sight, and Sound*. Free Press, 2005.

RIES A. and RIES L. *The Fall of Advertising & The Rise of PR*. HarperBusiness, 2002.

ROSEN E. *The Anatomy of Buzz, How to Create Word-of-mouth Marketing*. Currency, 2000.

SACHARIN K. *Attention! How to interrupt, yell, whisper, and touch consumers…* (Adweek Book series) John Wiley & Sons, 2001.

SAUNDERS J. *Communications Challenge, a Practical Guide to Media Neutral Planning*. The Account Planning Group, 2004.

SCHMITT BERND H. *Experiential Marketing. How to get customers to sense, feel, think, act, relate to your company and brands*. Free Press, 1999.

WIPPERFÜRTH A. *Brand Hijack. Marketing without Marketing*. Portfolio, 2005.

ZYMAN S. *The End of Advertising As We Know It*. John Wiley & Sons, 2002.

Articles

AAKER DAVID A. and JOACHIMSTHALER E. 'Building Brands Without Mass Media.' *Harvard Business Review*, Jan–Feb 1997.

ASTHANA A. 'How graffiti artists are cleaning up.' *The Observer*, 15 August 2004.

ATKINSON C. 'TV Ad-skipping Losses to Hit $27 Billion over Five Years.' *AdAge*, 14 April 2005.

ATKINSON C. 'Broadcast TV Networks Rattled by DVR Inroads.' *AdAge*, 11 April 2005.

BLOOM J. 'Wrestling Marketers Down to Naked Reality.' *AdAge*, 21 March 2005.

BLOOM J. 'In Search of a New Agency Model.' *AdAge*, 7 March 2005.

BURROWES T. and GOLF C. 'TV Advertising is dying, claims marketing guru.' *Media Week*, 25 September 2003.

BYRNES N., BERNER R., ZELLNER W., SYMONDS, W. 'Branding: Five New Lessons.' *BusinessWeek*, 14 February 2005.

CARTER, M. 'Remote control over audiences.' *The Financial Times*, 8 February 2005, p. 4.

CHERRY L. 'Posters Power Profits.' *Toronto Star*, 18 October 1999.

CLOTHIER J. 'The Changing Face of Advertising.' *CNN*, 12 August 2004.

CORR A. 'Product Placement: Agencies Debate Next Steps.' *Mediapost Communications*, 24 September 2004.

CRAIN R. 'Why Established Methods of Advertising Are the Answer.' *AdAge*, 14 March 2005.

CUNEO ALICE Z. 'Nissan plays with fire.' *AdAge*, 11 October 2004.

CUTHBERT W. 'Mainstream Advertisers Go Wild in the Streets.' *Strategy Magazine*, 27 September 1999.

DE CHENECEY S. 'The New Persuaders.' *Admap*, September, 2000.

DONATON S. 'Why We Must Forge Ahead Into New Ways of Advertising.' *AdAge*, 14 March 2005.

EISENBERG D., MCDOWELL J., BERESTEIN L., TSIANTAR D., FINAN E. 'It's an Ad, Ad, Ad, Ad World.' *Time*, 9 February 2002.

FELDENKRIS A. 'Can't We All Just Get Along?' *Brand New World*, October 11, 2004.

FITZGERALD K. 'While media factories trot out cool tools, some shops soar via planning's creative side.' *AdAge*, 11 February 2002.

FOLB M. 'Corporations Do the Wild Thing.' *Marketing Magazine*, 27 April 1999.

GREEN J. and KHERMOUCH G. 'Buzz Marketing, Suddenly this Stealth Strategy is Hot – but it's still Fraught with Risk.' *BusinessWeek*, 30 July 2001.

HALL E. and MADDEN N. 'Ikea's Global Reach Bows to Local Culture.' *AdAge*, 12 April 2004.

HEINZL J. 'Mainstream Advertisers Go Wild for Wild Postings.' *The Globe and Mail*, 22 March 2002.

HORYN C. 'Fashion houses going "guerrilla".' *The New York Times*, 17 February 2004.

IRWIN R. 'Street Level Strategy.' *Brandchannel*, 5 July 2004.

JURGENSEN J. 'The Underhanded Pitch.' *Courant*, 4 February 2005.

KAIKATI ANDREW M. and KAIKATI JACK G. 'Stealth Marketing: How to Reach Consumers Surreptitiously.' *California Management Review*, Summer 2004, vol. 46, no. 4.

KAYE K. 'Sales Pitch Society, how advertisers get us to do their dirty work.' *The Lowbrow Lowdown*, 2001. http://www.salespitchsociety.com

LEONARD D. 'Nightmare on Madison Avenue.' *Fortune*, 28 June 2004.

LEVY S. 'The Alpha Bloggers.' *Newsweek*, 20 December 2005.

LINDSTROM M. 'Turn Customers Into Marketers.' *Clickz.com*, 22 April 2003.

MACARTHUR K. and CHURA H. 'Urban Warfare.' *AdAge*, 4 September 2000.

MACDONALD G. 'What's In It For Me?' *Contagious*, October 2004, pp 38–41.

MANLY L. 'The Future of the 30-second Spot' *The New York Times*, 27 March 2005.

MARKILLIE P. 'Target Practice. Advertising used to be straightforward, now it has to be many different things to different people.' *The Economist*, 2 April 2005.

MEDIAEDGE:CIA. 'Connecting with the new consumer. The case for a new approach to brand communication', 2002.

MINOW N. 'Have you heard?' *Chicago Tribune*, 21 September 2004.

NEFF J. 'P&G sends in troupes to fight laundry wars.' *AdAge*, 15 May 2000.

PICCALO G. 'The Pitch that you won't see coming.' *Chicago Tribune*, 22 August 2004.

ROSE F. 'The Lost Boys.' *Wired*, August 2004.

SANDERS L. 'More marketers have to go to the bathroom.' *AdAge*, 20 September 2004.

Credits

SANGHERA S. 'Can Matthew Freud be serious?' *The Financial Times*, 2 December 2001.

SAUER A. 'Ambush Marketing Steals the Show.' *Brandchannel*, 27 May 2002.

SAUNDERS J. 'Back to the Future (With a Difference).' *Admap*, May 2002.

SCHULMAN A. 'The New Creative Imperative.' *Brand New World*, 18 August 2004.

SENNOTT S. 'Gone in 30 seconds.' *Newsweek International*, 23 February 2004.

SYRETT M. 'The Tragedy of the Advertising Commons.' *MarketingProfs*, September 2004.

TEMPLE J. 'Ads flying "under the radar".' *San Francisco Business Times*, 6 September 2002.

THOMPSON S. 'Targeting teens means building buzz.' *AdAge*, 27 March 2000.

VILBIG P. 'Advertising's sneak.' *The New York Times Upfront*, 4 August 2002.

WALKER R. 'The Hidden (in Plain Sight) Persuaders.' *The New York Times*, 5 December 2004.

WOLF B. 'All the World's an Ad.' *ABC News*, 12 March 2004.

Thanks

To my brother Matthias, who helped me to harass agencies and advertisers for several months; to Jan Wittouck for his advice and presence in crucial moments; to Tom Theys for his smart feedback and for helping me to steal some ads in Cannes; to Duval Guillaume Brussels for giving me some time off before I ran away; to mortierbrigade for their support and enthusiasm; to my parents for always being there; and to all others who gave their input or sent campaigns.

List of campaigns ordered alphabetically by agency within chapters

Installation

Campaign	Page	Agency	Client
107	104	BSUR	Wrangler
101	99	Crispin Porter + Bogusky	Mini Cooper
106	102	Cunning	Maryland Cookies
104	100	DM9DDB	Clorox
105	102	Hall & Cederquist/Y&R	Kraft Foods
103	100	Jung von Matt	The Protestant Church
97	97	New Deal DDB	IKEA
91	93	Ogilvy & Mather, Rightford Searle-Tripp & Makin	City of Cape Town
100	98	Saatchi & Saatchi	Childline India Foundation
109	105	Springer & Jacoby	DaimlerChrysler
96	96	Strawberry Frog	IKEA
99	98	Strawberry Frog	Interbrew
94	94	TBWA\Chiat Day	Absolut Vodka
92	94	TBWA\Germany	Absolut Vodka
95	95	TBWA\Germany	Absolut Vodka
93	94	TBWA\London	Absolut Vodka
102	99	TBWA\Singapore	Mini Cooper
98	97	Ubi Bene	IKEA
108	104	Universal McCann	Washington Mutual Home Loans

Illusion

Campaign	Page	Agency	Client
128	121	Advico Young &Rubicam	Hakle-Kimberly Switzerland GmbH
110	107	Age Comunicação	MTV
134	125	Almap BBDO	Senna Import
118	114	BBDO Argentina	Nike
112	108	BBDO Hong Kong	ING
142	133	ClaydonHeeleyJonesMason	PlayStation
133	125	Colenso BBDO	Environment Waikato
148	138	Colenso BBDO	TV3
145	136	Crispin Porter + Bogusky	Mini
156	145	Crispin Porter + Bogusky	Mini
111	108	DDB	Reporters Without Borders
147	137	DDB New Zealand	nzgirl
159	147	The Dukes of Urbino.com	Department of Transport
124	117	Hakuhodo	Ajinomoto Co./Knorr
152	142	Hakuhodo	The Mainichi Newspaper
140	130	Jung von Matt	International Foundation of Human Rights
155	144	Jung von Matt	Sixt
113	109	The Jupiter Drawing Room	Nedbank
129	121	The Jupiter Drawing Room	Foschini
149	139	J Walter Thompson Malaysia	Channel 9
120	115	Leo Burnett GmbH	Amnesty International
117	113	M&C Saatchi	Zuji
146	136	Master JWT	Brazilian Ministry of Health

Campaign	Page	Agency	Client
127	120	McCann-Erickson	Purina
130	122	Mediaedge:CIA	Warner Bros.
139	129	Mediaedge:CIA	IKEA
144	135	mortierbrigade	Le Soir
121	115	Naked Communications	Abbey
158	146	Network BBDO	Delta Motor Corporation
131	123	Ogilvy & Mather	Nike
151	141	Ogilvy & Mather	The Economist
153	143	Ogilvy & Mather	Nike
114	110	Prisma Propaganda	Real Café
150	140	Publicis Mojo	Paton Fertilizers
123	117	Rethink Communications	Trim Line
116	112	Saatchi & Saatchi	AXN
119	114	Saatchi & Saatchi	Guinness UDV
157	145	Saatchi & Saatchi	New Zealand Post
135	126	Scholz & Friends	German Initiative to Ban Landmines
122	116	Springer & Jacoby Werbung	Mercedes-Benz
125	118	Springer & Jacoby	DaimlerChrysler
126	119	Springer & Jacoby	DaimlerChrysler
137	128	Springer & Jacoby Media	T-Mobile
132	124	TBWA\Hunt Lascaris	SABC 2
115	111	TBWA\Paris	Amora
138	128	TBWA\Paris	SNCF
141	131	TBWA\Paris	Responsible Young Drivers
136	127	Ubi Bene	Nike
143	134	Wieden + Kennedy	Sega
154	144	Zig	Unilever Canada

Infiltration

Campaign	Page	Agency	Client
168	155	Cunning	British Airways
171	158	Cunning	Mini Cooper
161	150	Fathom Communications	Sony Ericsson Mobile Communications Ltd
160	149	Grey Worldwide Chile	Carabineros de Chile
162	150	Leo Burnett Chile	Procter & Gamble
172	159	Lowe	Sire
164	152	Maverick	UIP
164	152	Mediaedge:CIA	UIP
170	157	Network BBDO	Ceres Fruit Juices
166	154	Ogilvy & Mather	The Economist
165	153	Publicis Salles Norton	Gafisa
163	151	Street Attack	Dunlop
173	160	TBWA\Frederick	Recalcine Laboratory
167	154	TBWA\Hunt Lascaris	Nando's
169	156	Universal McCann	SSL International
174	161	Young &Rubicam	Hard Rock Hotel Chicago